A DEVIL FROM THE BEGINNING

THE ANTICHRIST REVEALED

ANTHONY J RITTHALER

A Devil From The Beginning
The Antichrist Revealed
by Anthony J Ritthaler

Printed in the United States of America

ISBN 9781612150130

Unless otherwise indicated, Bible quotations are taken from The King James Bible.

Noah Webster's Dictionary

www.xulonpress.com

Table of Contents

SPECIAL THANKS

There are several people that I want to thank for their influence concerning this book. I will get to them in a minute. However, first and foremost I want to thank my Savior, the Lord Jesus Christ. Ever since I have been saved, His hand has helped and guided me in every situation. He has been my best friend during that time. I remember, after I met Jesus as a teenager, it seemed as though every time I would think about doing wrong or entertaining the opportunity to run with the wrong crowd, God would always deal with me, and use His sweet Holy Ghost to convict me, and show me that what I was doing was wrong. It is safe to say that without Jesus as my friend and guide, I would be no where near where I am today. I will confess to you with a pure heart that when everybody else will forsake you, if you are saved, you have a friend that "sticketh closer than a brother," and Jesus will never forsake you. I often sing a song in church entitled, "I'll Not Turn My Back on Him Now," and I mean that with all my heart. Jesus has been so good to me throughout the course of my life and there is no doubt that I deserve none of it. If Jesus closed the windows of heaven and refused to shower any more blessings down upon me, I would still have to praise His Holy Name because He died on the cross for me. That is enough as far as I'm concerned. There have been many nights in my life that I have been alone and depressed about circumstances that have come my way, and I wondered if I would ever make it through. It was at that exact moment that Jesus would comfort me through the reading of His Word, the songs of Zion, or the preaching of His Word. In just a matter of minutes, I would go from being sad to being glad. Before I knew it, I would be filled with the Holy Ghost and running around the house through His presence that over shadowed me. There is a verse in the Bible that is so true. The verse says, "Without me, ye can do nothing." This is referring to Jesus. There is nothing more true than that statement. Jesus means the world to me, and I'm not afraid to say it.

When I set out to write this book, there was literally nobody I knew that believed what I did concerning this subject. Everybody that I knew was taught that Judas could not be the Antichrist, and if you ever suggested this to them they would laugh at you and say you were crazy. The problem is that they had no scripture for what they believed. I remember talking to certain people about this book and they would never think twice about the subject. Even after all of this, Jesus would speak to my heart and tell me that this was right. God would give me verse after verse and thought after thought. Before I knew it, He had given me so much material concerning this subject that it led to the writing of this book. No matter what others would say, Jesus would say more. I stand amazed that Jesus would use someone such as me, but yet He does. Jesus is the best friend a man could ever hope to find and He can guide you along life's road. Within myself I have very little ability but, with the help of Jesus,

I can do great things[1]. If you don't know Jesus, please accept Him today and you will find out for yourself what I am talking about.

I also want to thank the two most spiritual people in my life. They have loved me, provided me with a good Christian home, and protected me from this wicked world throughout my entire life. I am speaking about my Mom and Dad. Without their love and support I would probably be on my way to hell today. Instead, I am serving God and on my way to heaven through their prayers and dedication to the cause of Christ. For as long as I can remember, they have been on fire for the service of God. They raised me in a great church and took me every time the doors were open. Their impact on my life is unexplainable, and I thank God for them. Growing up, I made a hard decision to avoid the things of this world and follow Christ no matter how hard it would be. In that decision, it cost me a lot of so-called friends and many worldly experiences. That led to a lot of lonely times and quiet moments.

Through it all, when seemingly all had forsaken and turned their back on me, I still had my mom and the presence of God. My mom

---

[1] Philippians 4:13

has been my best friend (outside of Jesus, of course), and I praise God everyday for her. My mom and I have shared things with each other that nobody else knows about. In my opinion, she is in the top five spiritual women in the world. She is such a hard worker in the service of God, and the amount of work she has performed throughout her years in church amazes me. My mom is afflicted with so many physical troubles in her life, that naming them all would probably fill the rest of this book. However, thank God it has never stopped her from teaching Sunday school, driving a bus to pick up children for church, or even helping others that may be less fortunate. My mom is a great example for Christ and one day she will be rewarded greatly by the Savior. Words cannot describe the mother I have, so I will simply give you God's words to describe her. In the Proverbs 31:10-31, the Bible describes a virtuous woman and how they are rare and hard to find. They are special and old-fashioned in their beliefs. They are priceless and far above rubies. For everyone that knows my mom, they would agree that the Bible defines her perfectly.

I also want to thank my dad for all that he means to me. My dad has served the Lord since before I was born. His dedication to the things of God has always impressed me. We have had a wonderful time together serving the Lord, and he has taught me a great deal. His testimony of salvation stirs my soul whenever I'm blessed to hear it. He has helped me so much concerning this book, and I couldn't have done it without him. My dad has been a deacon, a teacher, a help to the man of God, and a great father. He taught me at a young age to respect the things of God and take them very seriously. Even to this day, I have never played around in the House of God and it has benefited me greatly. Through Dad's council, I have learned to get alone with God and to hear his still, small voice as he speaks to my heart.

Without my mom and dad to guide me in the things of God, I would most likely be away from God and out of His will. My dad's favorite verse is found in Hebrews 10:31 where it says, "It's a fearful thing to fall into the hands of a living God." I have never forgotten that and I never will. Thank you, Mom and Dad, for your service to Jesus Christ all these years. When I think of the impact you have made on my life, only one verse comes to my mind. It is the verse in the Book of Proverbs 22:6 that says, "Train up a child in the way that he should go and when he is old he will not depart from it." My goal has always been to make you proud of me through my walk with God, and I sure hope I have.

Another person I want to thank is my wife, Erin. The Bible says that a good wife is hard to find. My wife is a good, Godly woman that has gone through a lot lately and has supported me to the best of her ability. She has been a part of Hope Baptist Church since she was a baby and has stayed faithful to Christ all her life. I stand amazed at her abilities and I'm so thankful that she is my wife. Her pastor and his wife – Timothy and Bonnie Ammon – love her to death and are so grateful for her service to the church. She is the piano player and has been for some time. Thank You, Erin, for your love and support during this process. I hope I can be a good husband to you for years to come and our new baby, Hope Ann. I look forward to serving

Christ with you in the future and loving God together as we live the rest of our lives with one another.

There are so many preachers and teachers I've heard that have made an impact on my life throughout the course of my years in church. I want to say that I'm so thankful for every one of them. With that being said, there are three preachers that have stood above the rest when it comes to changing my life and teaching me the things of God.

First of all, I want to thank Dr. Lawrence Mendez. He is the pastor of Open Door Baptist Church in Detroit, Michigan. My family and I had the joy of being members of his church for five years. In that time we learned things about the Bible that some people would only dream about. Dr. Mendez is one of the great Bible preachers of our day, and without his impact on my life I really don't know where I would be. Dr. Mendez always teaches his members some-thing very important about studying the Bible. He taught us never to be in a race to rush through the Bible, but rather to make sure you understand a verse before you move on to another. He taught us to take our time when we read the Bible, even if it takes us all day to understand that verse. Meditating on a verse is extremely important when reading. You must ask God to open up the Word to you when you study it, rather than racing through its pages to impress the brethren. Dr. Mendez is, no doubt, a spiritual giant and a great friend. Often when working on this book, verses would come into my mind that would prove the point I was trying to make. The reason verses would come so easily was because of the Holy Ghost, of course, but also because of the method that Dr. Mendez taught me to study the Word of God – verse by verse and to implant scriptures deep inside my heart. Thank you so much, Dr. Mendez, for staying faithful to the things of God and for being a good example for me to follow. You have been like a big brother to me and have helped me immensely with this book.

The second man of God that I would personally like to thank for his influence on my life would have to be Dr. Phil Kidd of Amory, Mississippi. Dr. Kidd, in my opinion, is the greatest preacher of our generation. He has preached over fourteen thousand times in the thirty-four years of his Christian life. His ministry has touched untold thousands of people worldwide. Heaven only knows the difference he has made for the cause of Christ, and I believe the judgement seat of Christ will prove that.[2] I can remember the first time I saw Dr. Kidd at Open Door Baptist Church. The truth was I had only heard Dr. Kidd preach by way of CD and tape, but had never seen what he actually looked like before. I recall seeing Dr. Kidd for the first time and knowing that it was him simply by viewing the power of God that he was exhibiting by his appearance. It reminded me of a bible character and up to that point I had never seen anything like that before. The Lord laid it on my heart to help him in anyway I could, and he has, no doubt, returned that favor towards me. Dr. Kidd has showed so much kindness and love towards me that it is, without question, a humbling experience. Dr. Kidd travels this country and preaches nearly every day of his life the gospel of Jesus Christ. He is probably the busiest evangelist in America today, but he is never too busy to help a fellow Christian in need. I want to thank him for his stand for Christ, and what he has meant to America, in his

---

[2] II Corinthians 5:10

thirty-four years of Christian service. One of the best decisions that I have ever made, as a young man, was when I decided to purchase hundreds of Dr. Kidd's messages to learn more about the Word of God. Dr. Kidd is such a powerful man of God and it is refreshing to hear preaching like his in such a wicked generation as that of the one we are living in. If you love God and want to hear a spirit-filled man of God preach the Word, then I suggest you visit Dr. Kidd's website and invest in some of his preaching items that he has available to the public. Take it from me, you will not be disappointed and it may be the best decision you will ever make (short of salvation). I have heard nearly every one of his messages and some over and over again. My personal favorites would have to be the following: "A Glimpse of Glory; The Root of Rebellion; Be My Guest to the Depths of Hell; The Ministry of Repentance," and his personal testimony story. Dr. Kidd is the D.L.Moody of this generation and I'm so thankful that our paths crossed many years ago. I want to thank him for his influence on my life and his impact on America. Thank you, Dr. Kidd, from the bottom of my heart.

The last preacher that I would like to thank is none other than Pastor Timothy Ammon of Romulus, Michigan. My respect for Pastor Ammon cannot be measured. In my opinion, he is the Noah of our day. It seems like the bigger the crowd, the harder he preaches. Much like Noah, his crowd is small, but his doctrine is unmatched. Pastor Ammon is old-fashioned, and a King James (1611 A.D.) only man. Pastor has a love for his people that is felt and respected by all. The reason Pastor Ammon reminds me so much of Noah is because he is more concerned about telling you the truth and having a small crowd if necessary, than to compromise or lie in order to gain a large crowd. Pastor Ammon refuses to trick a man or woman down a church aisle like so many preachers do in this day, but will rather preach the truth, hang them out over hell, and let the chips fall where they may. He loves God with all his heart and refuses to change his stand on the Word of God, much like Noah. Pastor Ammon does not have a large crowd, but he has some of the best members a pastor could ever hope to have. I have the utmost respect for this great servant of God, and inspire to be just like him in the years to come.

He has been a great leader and example for Hope Baptist Church for many years, and everyone that knows him will testify that this is true. Pastor Ammon has always been one of my heroes of the faith, and someone I could always look up to. Thank you so much, Pastor Ammon, for staying with God all these years, and preaching the truth to a dying world. You have definitely been through hardships and disappointments in your years as a Christian, but you have never wavered once, as far as I can tell. You are so unique and so rare in this generation. I pray that you will remain faithful to the cause of Christ – and keep on keeping on. Your importance to the work of the Lord is so great and your reward will be also. Thank you for being a pastor that we can lean on and serve God with in a crooked and perverse generation. Please don't ever change, you are great just as you are.

Last but not least, I want to thank all the people that may purchase a copy of this book. Without the support of the people, writers would have nothing. It takes men, women, boys, and girls to show interest in a book to make it succeed. This may be a good book, but without your love and support, it would only be a belief of mine and not a reality. Spreading the news about this book will cause others to be aware of whom the Antichrist is. I had a vision when I wrote this book to inform as many people as I could of who Judas Iscariot is and has always been. With your help, we can help many people worldwide. Thank you so much for your interest in this book. I hope that God will speak to your heart about this subject and change your view on the Antichrist, forever. Without your help it cannot succeed and I hope God blesses you in the future. Thank you once again.

Bro. Tony

INTRODUCTION

I would like to say right from the start that I am dealing with a very debatable subject in this book, and one that I know will draw various opinions from many people. I am twenty-eight years old and have been in church my entire life. I have had the privilege of hearing so many great men of God and have probably heard more preaching than anyone my age in this generation. I have literally heard thousands of preaching tapes and CD's of good Bible teachers and preachers of the Gospel. Never have I dropped out of church or gone the way of the world. I used to go home after church and get alone with God and listen to ten or twelve preaching messages a night. This helped me learn more about the Bible and grow closer to Jesus.

That being said, I have only heard one man of God in my entire life agree with the subject matter I am dealing with in this book. I know for a certainty that when I approached my family and told them that I was writing a book and of its particular subject matter, I received mixed reactions. At one point I noted some laughter because of the straight, Biblical way I have been taught. I am certain that when you first hear the book's subject you will, without a doubt, have various thoughts or ideas which are contrary to my view.

At the very start I had a difficult time convincing myself that this was wholly accurate as well. Needless to say, I believe the Word of God is the final authority and the only thing that truly matters. I am definitely going against the grain and what many great men believe on this topic. I say, "...Let God be true but every man a liar.[3]" It does not matter what man believes - it matters what the Word of God says!

The subject I am writing about is simply <u>who the antichrist is</u>. It is my feeling that many Bible scholars believe as I do, only they do not have enough scripture or facts to support their conviction. Let

[3] Romans 3:4

me tell you that as you read this book, you will identify that I have both. There is so much scripture involved in this book that it will probably shock you. Many times as I went through my daily routine, I would be studying on this topic at work when God would give me a thought and I would immediately jot it down so that it wouldn't be forgotten. The Lord has helped me so much with the writing of this book. I want to say that He deserves all the glory. It is my prayer that throughout the course of reading this book, God will open your eyes as He did mine and show you that what you believe may not necessarily be accurate. It is wrong if it does not line up with the Bible, no matter how good it may sound. I would never write a book like this and publish it to the world if I did not have the scripture to back it up.

The person that I am convinced is the antichrist was one of Jesus Christ's closest disciples and someone he was very familiar with[4]. There is very little written of this man in the Bible and what *is* written, is not good. It seems that his whole life was designed for one purpose. He was pure evil and always had a hidden plan or

---

[4] Psalm 41:9

agenda, unlike the other disciples. This man was so wicked that not even the common dog bears his name today. He always knew what to do or say at the right time and had much charisma. Jesus said that this man was a devil and foreknew that he would be betrayed by him, long before it ever happened. The man that I believe is the antichrist is none other than Judas Iscariot, himself.

As you read, I want you to notice just how similar Judas' life was to that of the antichrist. While I was compiling this book, all of the verses and thoughts just seemed to flow and work together in perfect harmony. Some things written in this book are undeniable and surprising. With all of the important facts and pure Bible, I feel that this editorial will grab your attention. I have always believed that Judas was more than just a man who betrayed the Lord and went to hell. There are various passages in the Bible that Jesus, Himself said that we need to take note of, and many of these verses throughout the scriptures are stunning when you take the time to read them.

Judas Iscariot is a predestined man, just as the antichrist is, which will be seen as you read. He was straight out of Hell and a reprobate, also as the antichrist is. There are so many facts concerning Judas and the antichrist that are so precisely the same, I am convinced they will jump right out at you. Judas went to his own place when he died, just as the antichrist will do after he dies in the tribulation period. I believe that your eyes will open as you begin to see how things that you were always taught do not match up with the Bible. I would never write a book about such a serious subject if I did not feel it was important. I feel that people should know the truth about who Judas really was. He was on a mission to complete his lifelong goal and nothing was going to stop him. The majority of what is written is not my opinion, but Biblical fact, based on the truth of the Word of God, and so I feel that it will be nearly impossible to argue with the content of this book. I do not wish to sit in church and hear false teaching about Judas and the antichrist again.

I would never write a book on this subject for personal gain or fame. I have always tried to aid or support the man of God and the church in my Christian service to Jesus. Having given nearly all my earnings to support the cause of Christ, this would be no different in that nearly all my proceeds would go to His cause and glory.

I assure you that I was on a mission to finish this book for two reasons. The main motivation came about as I studied and the verses seemed to come alive. I realized that Jesus wanted us to know the truth about the antichrist, or this man named Judas Iscariot. Throughout this book, we are able to see distinctive things that Jesus gave Christians concerning this man named Judas. The second cause for finishing this book is due to the simple fact that the return of Jesus could occur any day. If you are familiar with the end times or the things written in the Bible, you will quickly see that our time is short. Jesus compares the last days to those of Noah and Lot. Looking around at this world, you will easily see a striking resemblance. If you read Matthew 24, Mark 13, and II Timothy 3, you will find that it would be like reading the daily newspaper. We, Christians understand that we are just about to pull out of here and be caught up in the rapture to meet Jesus. It is because of these two reasons alone that I felt a need to make this book available.

I will also discuss briefly who I believe the fore-runner (or set-up man) to the antichrist will be. Just as John the Baptist was a fore-runner for Jesus in proclaiming that the Messiah was on his way, the Devil will also have a fore-runner to set things in motion for the coming of the antichrist. We are seeing this even as I write and it is very alarming to us that understand the Bible. The reason I believe this is because everything that God originates, the devil imitates. If you know your history, then you know that this is true. The Bible teaches that what God has set up, the Devil attempts to imitate or simulate (this is seen later in the book).

I would like to express to you that this book is not only for the Christian, but for the non-Christian as well. I believe that this book is, for the most part, written for both the saved and the unsaved. I want the saved and lost alike to understand who the antichrist is. If you are lost and do not know Jesus Christ as your personal Savior, I beg you to "get right" with God before it is too late. Please allow God speak to you through this book, for time is running out. As I was taking notes and preparing this book, I would share with fellow workers what God was showing me about Judas. Most of the people, who don't go to church, told me how amazing and eye-opening they thought it was. One lady called me "Nostradamus" and said that I needed to finish this book. To that I say, I am no Nostradamus, but the Bible does not lie.

In Hebrews 4:12, the Bible describes the Word of God as, "... quick, and powerful, and sharper than any twoedged sword." As you read, you will see the Word of God describing Judas in a way you may have never seen before. My goal in this book is to make you a believer, and to cause you to see how the Word of God meant for us to view this man named Judas Iscariot. The Bible says in II Timothy 2:15, "Study to shew thyself approved unto God, a workman that needeth not to be ashamed, rightly dividing the word of truth." It also says in II Timothy 3:16, "All scripture is given by inspiration of God, and is profitable for doctrine, for reproof, for correction, for instruction in righteousness." We are instructed in John 5:39 to search the scriptures.

In conclusion, all I want you to do while reading this book is to match it up with the Bible and compare it to the scriptures. If you will do so, then you will see the truth about Judas Iscariot and the antichrist, and will have an entirely new view on the subject, just as I do. Please do not trust man's opinion, but believe in the Word of God, the King James (1611 A.D.), Authorized Version of the Bible. I personally would like to thank you for reading this book and I hope you enjoy the ride. May God bless you as you read.

THE UNHOLY TRINITY

There is one important factor about the Bible and this book that I would like to establish from the very beginning, and that is to bring to your attention the foundation of <u>why I believe that Judas was different from other men and why he was sent to be the Son of Perdition, or the Antichrist.</u> The Bible clearly teaches that just as there is a Holy Trinity (found in I John 5:6-8), there is also an unholy trinity found throughout the entire Bible. This is clearly established in Revelation 20:10 and Revelation 16:13. Throughout this book I will show you many reasons why Judas Iscariot was more than just a normal man and, without doubt, part of this unholy trinity.

In the beginning of time, before man was ever created, God enjoyed the praise of Lucifer and the heavenly host in the heaven that he had created. Their entire purpose of existence was to honor God and sing praises unto the Father, Son, and Holy Ghost until the end of time. God loved His creation and designed them to dwell with Him for all eternity in the glory of heaven. Lucifer, however, began to ponder within his heart what it would be like to excel above God, and to figure out how to dethrone his Maker.

God had other plans, as we know, and with a broken heart had to create a place called Hell that was "prepared for the Devil and his angels.[1]" As a result of sin and rebellion, not only was Lucifer banished from the presence of God, but also a third of the angels that followed the Devil were sentenced to a lifetime of pain and suffering in the pits of the damned. From that moment on, the Devil went from Lucifer (which means beautiful), to Satan or the Devil (which means "the prince of darkness or deceiver[2]). Even since before the fall of man there has been - and throughout eternity there always will be - a battle between good and evil.

Everything that God originates, the Devil will continually imitate. Just as there is a Holy Trinity that is ordained to be holy and good, there also is an unholy trinity which was born through sin and rebellion, meant to be evil and satanic. Ever since Lucifer's fall in the beginning by transgression, God made him a reprobate from that point forward. In other words, Satan's whole purpose for existing is to fulfill his title and to cause other men and women to rebel against the things of God. Everything God tries to establish in this world for good, Satan tries to destroy or corrupt. God is not capable of lying or sinning because He is holy and just[3]. Satan, on the other hand, is unable to tell the truth or do right because he is of the unholy trinity[4]. You will see this throughout the study as we uncover Judas' life.

From the start of the Bible until the end, you will find that everywhere the Holy Trinity is working to redeem man back to God or to do right, the unholy trinity is present to cause confusion and rebellion in the heart of men. I will give you a few examples of this. In the Book of Genesis, chapters one through three, you will find that God created men in his own image[5]. He created man as perfect and free

33

from sin in the beginning of time. He desired to walk with Adam and have sweet fellowship in the cool of the day. As we know, the Devil came and tempted Adam's wife, Eve, and caused her to partake of the fruit. Adam also took of the fruit after God had already forbidden them. When Adam disobeyed and took of the fruit, he became a sinner and caused all of mankind to become sinners as well. Here we are able to see the unholy trinity at work even from the start of mankind. The Devil cannot stand God and wants to steal all his glory.

I also think about Cain and Abel. Abel was a righteous man who only wanted to please God through a blood sacrifice. Cain, on the other hand, was a man that was full of the Devil and hated even the presence of a righteous soul. Satan filled Cain with so much anger and rebellion that he arose and killed his only brother, simply because he was trying to do right. We see again another example of good against evil in the life of these two brothers.

When you come to the days of Noah you will find that the Devil was almost in complete control of the hearts and minds of the people through wicked imaginations and sinful lusts. Noah was a preacher of righteousness and damnation. He walked with God and preached for one hundred and twenty years. In that time period of warning and pleading with the hearts of men, literally only eight people believed Noah and tried to do right. The remaining people followed the Devil's highway and were destroyed by the flood.

It's amazing how fast the unholy trinity moved to defile the hearts of men. In just the first six chapters of the Book of Genesis, from when God created man to walk in His way, the Devil had already polluted the minds of the world's people. God had no choice but to wipe them off the face of the earth and start over again. The Bible says in I Peter 5:8 that the Devil walketh about seeking whom he may devour. It is called the unholy trinity. The Word of God is filled with examples of good against evil. When you enter into the beginning stages of the Bible, you will find that rebellion was constantly controlling the hearts of the people.

I think about when Moses was getting the Ten Commandments from God Himself, on top of the mountain. Moses was trying to walk with God and be the leader of the children of Israel. In just a short period of time, the Devil was working to destroy all of what God was trying to put in place. With the glow of God on his face, Moses came down from the mountain and saw his people dancing naked around a golden calf, disobeying the Lord's commands. All throughout the Bible you will find the Devil fighting to destroy what God meant for good.

Through the first portion of the Bible you will find much demon activity being performed and Satan trying to oppose God in every way possible. Towards the middle of the Old Testament you will find the Devil still opposing the authority of God. When you reach chapter one of the Book of Job, you find a man that is totally sold out to the service of God. Job loved God with all of his heart and was pure in the sight of Him. However, once again we find Satan appearing before God and asking for permission to cause pain unto this servant. The Lord knew Job's heart and, knowing all things, allowed Satan to have his way with Job. Needless to say, Satan tried his best to destroy the man of God with tragedy after tragedy. Through all his loss Job never yielded to the Devil's attack.

In the Book of Psalms we find Satan always fighting against King David and hoping to destroy his life. The Bible declares that David was the greatest king that Israel ever had and that he was a man after God's own heart. Jesus loved David so much that He chooses to sit on his throne during the tribulation period, as He rules and reigns for a thousand years. David was constantly attacked by the Devil because he loved God and tried to walk with Him.

Around the middle of the Old Testament we find the first mention of the Antichrist or the 'Man of Sin.' Amazingly, in that same chapter (one thousand years before he was born), Judas also appears in Psalms chapter fifty-five in comparison to the Antichrist. We will refer to this later in the book.

When we get to the end of the Old Testament, we will find Satan at work in the Book of Daniel. It is there in Daniel chapter three that the whole crowd was worshipping the image of Nebuchadnezzar. With pride, Satan had lifted him up and caused him to turn their hearts away from the God of their fathers. However the Bible tells us there were three Hebrew children that refused to bow to the image that had been set up. We understand that God appeared unto them in the midst of the fire and delivered them from the hands of death, thank the lord.[6]

There was also another man of God that was being greatly used to complete the plan of God. His named was Daniel. Satan hated Daniel simply because he had purposed in his heart to serve the Lord. No matter what Satan did to Daniel, God protected his servant, time after time. All through the pages of the Old Testament we see the Devil constantly working to destroy the foundation in which God had set up.

Near the end of the Old Testament, in the Book of Zechariah[7], we find that Judas and the Antichrist appear once again in the same chapter. This time, we find that Judas and the Antichrist is indeed the same person. Judas explains how just as he betrayed Jesus for thirty pieces of silver, he will also break the covenant that he established with all people in the tribulation period as the Antichrist. Judas Iscariot was not yet born when this was written. This portion of scripture clearly shows us that Judas and the Antichrist are, in fact, the same person and part of the unholy trinity.

When we come to the New Testament nothing changes but only intensifies. We read how God sends his only begotten Son, Jesus Christ into the world to die for the sins of the people as He was prophesied to do. When Jesus is born of a virgin and starts to live out his life as the Son of God, Bible scripture is being fulfilled on a daily basis. Jesus had to fulfill every scripture written of Him or his life would be a failure and He would cease to be God. Praise God, we understand that He fulfilled every scripture and lived a perfect life.

The Devil understood the plan of God and thought that if he could put enough pressure on the Son of God that maybe he could get Jesus to slip and cause Him to become a sinner. We know that the Devil in Matthew chapter 4 attacked the Son of God at His weakest point when Jesus was fasting for forty days and forty nights. Of course we understand that Jesus was God and He resisted the Devil and Satan had to leave Him. Much like God sent his best to fulfill His Holy Plan, the Devil also sent his best or his only son, Judas, to try to stop Jesus (which was Satan's *unholy* plan). As you will read in this book Judas was, in fact, the Devil's son and part of the unholy trinity – found in Revelation 20:10. Judas is labeled the Son of Perdition, or the man of sin. Jesus also called him a Devil and the power of darkness.

As you will read throughout the course of this book, you will see that Judas was never a help to Jesus but only a hindrance. The fact that he was the Devil's son shows us that he was a reprobate and unable to be saved. Never one time in the Bible will you find Judas under conviction of God to be saved. Jesus knew he was lost, but never once did He invite Judas to come to Him for salvation. There are major reasons for this. Because he was part of the unholy trinity and a reprobate, we understand that Judas had to fulfill Old Testament scriptures that were written about him. As you will read, because the scriptures can not be broken, Judas could never be saved because he had to betray the Lord for thirty pieces of silver just like the Bible said, or the Bible would be false. We know that Judas fulfilled all that was written of him because the Bible has no errors.

All throughout Jesus' ministry, Judas was sent to cause trouble for Jesus. Little is said about Judas and almost everything that is said is in a negative sense. Satan tried his best to put as much pressure on Jesus as he possibly could and he used his son Judas to do it. I believe it always weighed heavily on the mind of Jesus that His so-called friend Judas, whom he always tried to be good to, was a Devil the whole time and sent to betray Him. We find that Judas did his job perfectly. There was so much pressure on the shoulders of Jesus in the Garden of Gethsemane that the Bible declares He began to sweat great drops of blood. His soul was exceedingly sorrowful, even unto death[8]. What Judas was about to do broke the heart of Jesus, as it was a picture of things to come.

The unholy trinity was very much present during the ministry of Jesus. Satan did everything in his power to stop the Savior but to no avail, for Jesus died, arose the third day, and ascended back to heaven (just like the Bible said He would). When Judas completed his job, the Bible says he went back to his own place, referring to hell[9]. This fulfilled his description as the Son of Perdition or child of hell.

When we get to the middle of the New Testament we find a man by the name of Saul that was once working for the Devil but, in Acts chapter 9, we find that God calls him out of the kingdom of darkness and changed his life. Saul got saved and the Lord renamed him as 'Paul.' As the servant of Christ Paul tries, to the best of his ability, to serve Jesus with everything he has. However, Satan is always trying to hurt Paul and cause him to stumble until the day he dies.

Paul declares in Ephesians 6:10-17 that if you desire to walk with Jesus, the Devil will always try to attack you in every way. This is because you are a follower of Christ. Paul declares that we need to put on the whole armor of God that we may be able to withstand the wiles of the Devil. Paul also says in verse twelve that we are wrestling against principalities, powers, rulers of the darkness of this world, and against spiritual wickedness in high places. What Paul was telling us is that if you want to serve God, you will have to battle against evil. He over and over expresses to the world that much like there is a good side, there is an evil side as well. Paul was a part of both sides and so who better could explain the two trinities than Paul, himself?

As we come to the end of the New Testament we can truly see the unfolding of the unholy trinity like never before. In the book of Revelations, John the Beloved (inspired by God, Himself) wrote down everything he saw concerning the end times. As you will read in this book, the Antichrist will step on the scene with the False Prophet and the Devil – seemingly in full control. They will have all the answers for the first three and a half years of the Tribulation Period. However (much like Judas already displayed), the Antichrist will break his covenant and we will see the Devil in full control. His plan will be worked to perfection and all hell will break out on planet earth.

When the people have discovered that they have been deceived, it will be too late by this time. The unholy trinity will have full power and will rule through fear and domination. The Devil will then make the mistake of thinking that he is the God of the universe.

He will proclaim war against all that oppose him. The Devil will, by this time, have literally billions of followers that have devoted themselves to give him the glory that he has always desired. However, the Bible teaches in the Book of Revelation that exactly at this time the King of Kings and Lord of Lords will appear from heaven to meet him in the Battle of Armageddon. He will destroy him and his crowd with the "sword that proceedeth out of His mouth.[10]"

Finally, in Revelations 20:10 the unholy trinity is once and for all done away with when death and hell are cast into the Lake of Fire. Sin will be forever vanquished. At that time, there will be a new heaven and a new earth, and we will be with God for all eternity.

Just as there is a Holy Trinity that is Holy and Divine, there is also an unholy trinity that was a result of sin. The more you read this book, the more you will see that Judas is indeed the Antichrist and part of that unholy trinity.

It is really amazing how history always seems to repeat itself and, as you see the facts about Judas and the Antichrist, you will see that they are identical in nearly every way. I will bring you back to this fact and remind you that Judas is part of the unholy trinity throughout this book to further prove my point.

---

[1] Matthew 25:41
[2] Isaiah 14: 10-15
[3] II Corinthians 5:21
[4] John 8:44
[5] Genesis 1:26-27
[6] Daniel 3:25-26
[7] Zechariah 11: 10-14
[8] Matthew 26: 38-39
[9] Acts 1:25
[10] Revelations 19:15,21

JUDAS IN COMPARISON WITH THE ANTICHRIST

W hen you begin to look at the life and events of Judas Iscariot, your mind will quickly flash forward to the life of the Antichrist. Nobody is more similar in the Bible than these two men. There is a definite connection that these two men share that is stunning to say the least. There will be some things that I will list in this comparison that are seemingly identical. When you read the facts that are presented to you in this simple study, I believe you will view these two men like never before.

One thing that is common throughout this entire study of Judas and the Antichrist is the fact that Jesus, in John 17:12, calls Judas the "Son of Perdition." What's interesting about this title is the fact that no one else, in the entire Word of God, is called the Son of Perdition except the Antichrist himself. This is found in II Thessalonians 2:3. I do not want to dwell on this subject for too long, but the son of perdition simply means "child of damnation" or "man of sin". Later in the book we will discuss this.

Another thing that is similar between these two is the fact that the Bible declares they are straight out of hell. Again, I do not want to dwell on this subject forever because the book will go into great detail about this. In Acts 1:25 we find that when Judas died, it is clear that he went to "his own place," speaking of hell. The Bible says this about no other man except the Antichrist. You will find this in the Book of Revelations 20:10, after the unholy trinity is finished deceiving the world, when they will all be cast into their own place – the Lake of Fire.

What is also amazing and unique about these men is the fact that they are the only two lost men that ever are prophesied in the Old Testament which appear in the New Testament. They appear in the Old Testament many times and twice are mentioned in the same chapter of two different books. In Psalms chapter 55, you find Judas and the Antichrist being described by the Lord and even compared. In Zechariah, you will find Judas speaking as the Antichrist and describing how he was going to break his covenant with Israel, just like he had already broken his covenant with Jesus and betrayed him for thirty pieces of silver. The funny thing is that Judas was talking in the future, as the Antichrist and he wasn't even born yet.

Judas and the Antichrist are also predestinated men that are here to fulfill prophecy. They are the only two men that have ever lived or will live that were reprobates before they were even born. As a result of being part of the unholy trinity and blaspheming the Holy Ghost in the beginning of time, their fate was already sealed. Their sole purpose is to fulfill scripture and magnify themselves against God. I want you to study out your Bible and find one time when Jesus ever invited Judas or convicted him about his never-dying soul. You will never find it, nor will you ever find a time when Judas sought to be saved, or wanted God. Judas was prophesied to betray Him even before he was born. Once scripture is in place it cannot be broken.

You will see more of this explanation as you read the book. We all know the Antichrist will be evil, full of pride, and will never once turn from his sin and get saved, because he is a reprobate and the Man of Sin.

There are so many things that Judas and the Antichrist have in common when you sit down and think about it. Later in this book you will definitely see that, but I want to focus on some things that parallel these men together which you might have never really thought of before. I am a firm believer that history repeats itself, over and over again. If you know your history and your Bible, you know this to be true. History can be simply defined as "His-story," referring to Jesus Christ. For even time itself is based upon His life and death. Everything concerning the Bible and future events is centered on Israel – God's chosen people. When you break down these two words, you will find that "His-story" is real. I believe what God is showing us in the life of Judas, is a clear sign of what we can expect in the future. When you view the life of Judas and of the Antichrist, you will find that Judas set the stage and showed us what to look for when the Antichrist appears, repeating what he has already done.

The first thing that God was showing us through the life of Judas, was the fact that even though he was a lost man, Judas could perform miracles. This points to the fact that the Devil has the power to do amazing things as well, but that does not mean he'll go to heaven because he can perform miracles. Judas invented the modern day television evangelist, for what they do in this day and age is totally against the Word of God. They have the ability to deceive the people through lies, deception, and through many lying wonders and signs. Jesus warned us about these false preachers and teachers of the faith when he said in Matthew 7:21-23, "Not every one that saith Lord, Lord, shall enter into heaven, but he that doeth the will of God." In verse 22 he said, "Many will say to me in that day, Lord, Lord have we not prophesied in thy name, and in thy name have cast out devils, and in thy name done many wonderful works?" They are asking Jesus a question but he will say in verse 23, "I never knew you; depart from me, ye workers of iniquity." Just because people can do miracles does not mean that they know Jesus. We have proof of this in the life of Judas. He could perform miracles just like the other disciples in Matthew chapter 10, but he was still lost. The difference is that Judas was performing these miracles with the help of Satan, while the others were empowered by God. That is exactly what the Antichrist will use during the Tribulation Period.

In II Thessalonians 2:9-10, the Bible is clear that his coming is after the working of Satan, with all power, signs, lying wonders, and all deceivableness of unrighteousness in them that perish. Much like Judas, one of the Antichrist's tools will be this thing called miracles or signs and wonders.

The Jews were always asking Jesus to show them some kind of sign from heaven during his earthly ministry and Jesus had to tell them that a wicked and evil generation seeketh after a sign. The Jews would rather see some kind of miracle than anything else, and Jesus often rebuked them for it. Just like Judas could perform miracles to make himself seem more powerful than he really was, the Antichrist will follow the exact same pattern. He already knows exactly what the people are looking for and he will surely give it to them during the Tribulation Period. That is one thing that God was revealing to us through the life of Judas that you can look for in the Antichrist.

Another important factor that is the same between Judas and the Antichrist that God wanted us to know is the fact that they will both overflow with charisma. Nobody in the history of the world to this point has had a greater or larger amount of charisma, than Judas Iscariot did. Although Judas was a devil according John 6:70, I cannot find one place in the Bible where anybody, outside of Jesus, said anything bad or negative about Judas Iscariot before his betrayal. In fact, when Jesus announced that one of his disciples would betray him in Mark 14:18-19, the Bible records in the very next verse that no one thought it was Judas, but they all started to say,"Is it I? Is it I?" Judas had so much charisma and influence among his fellow disciples that even the greatest men on earth couldn't suspect anything wrong with this man. Charisma is a powerful thing. There are, without a doubt, people that have seemingly an extra amount of charisma than other people do. People that have charisma are able to influence others and get them to follow them, no matter if it is right or wrong.

Judas knew how to get people to notice him, and listen to what he had to say. Even though he was a thief, according to John 12:6, nobody ever knew he was stealing from God. Judas always thought one step ahead of everyone else, and literally had everyone fooled except God. The Bible says in II Corinthians 11:13-15 that "such are false apostles, deceitful workers, transforming themselves into the apostles of Christ." Does that sound like Judas or what? Verse 14 says, "No marvel, for Satan himself is transformed into an angel of light." Then it says, "…therefore, it is no great thing if his ministers also be transformed as the ministers of righteousness whose end shall be according to their works." May I say that when everyone looked at Judas with his or her natural eye, all they saw was an angel of light, when all the time he was a minister of Satan. Much like we have seen through the life of Judas already, the Antichrist will also be fair to look upon and will captivate the world through charisma. The Bible says in Psalms 55:21-23 that when the Antichrist comes on the scene he will not take over the world through force or violence at first, but through charisma and charm.

The Bible gave us an example already of what Judas used to win the hearts of the people and the Antichrist will do the same thing. In verse 21 of Psalms chapter 55, the Bible says, "His words are smoother than butter, but war is in his heart; His words were softer than oil, yet were they drawn swords." What we have seen in the life of Judas was a glimpse of things to come. As I said, history has a strange way of repeating itself and the Antichrist will seem perfect for a while, but all the time war is in his heart. It is something called charisma.

Another quality that ties these two together is the fact that they have a ministry of three and a half years before they are exposed and their true colors begin to show. In the life of Judas Iscariot, we see through the Bible that he arrives exactly when he is suppose to and he betrays Jesus exactly when he was suppose to. The timing of Judas constantly through out his three and a half year ministry has always been remarkable to me. I fully understand why Jesus knew the next step in God's Divine Plan, but it always seemed like Judas was always in the right place, at the right time as well. He fulfilled everything that was written about him, much like John the Baptist and Jesus did. This was because he was a man of destiny, according to the Old Testament scriptures. Like I said before, his first three and half years seemed nearly perfect, and nothing bad is ever said about him, beside the statements of Jesus. After three and a half years of being a liar is up, God flips on the light and pulls off the blanket, revealing to everyone who Judas was the whole time.

God was in control of this situation the entire time. When it was finally time to betray Jesus and fulfill his dream like the Bible teaches in John 13: 18-19, the Word of God declares that he was ready[1]. The Bible is teaching us through the life of Judas that the Antichrist will have three and half years of peace, as well. When those three and a half years of peace are up, the Antichrist will then break his covenant that he had set up with all the people, and you will see the power of darkness unfold before your very eyes. It's fascinating just how similar these chains of events seem to be when you speak of the two in comparison. In many cases concerning these two men, it is almost like looking in the mirror and viewing the same person. This is something to consider and think about.

When I start to view certain aspects of the betrayal of Jesus and how it took place, my mind begins to think of how similar the Tribulation Period will unfold and how God already has used the life of Judas to describe it. Just as the Antichrist is a predestinated man, so was Judas. Something that is very interesting about Judas is the fact that his timing was always perfect when it came to knowing the next step concerning the plan of God. Judas could have never been able to betray the Lord until Jesus finally said that the timing was right. You see, the Devil can not do anything without the approval of Jesus. God has this world under control and He knows the beginning from the end. Satan is on an eternal leash, like a dog.

Even though Satan is the ruler of the earth for a period of time, he still has to ask Jesus permission before he can do anything. When Satan wanted to test Job in the Old Testament, he had to ask God first. Another example of this was when Jesus was at His weakest point in His earthly ministry while fasting for forty days and nights, Satan tried to deceive and trick even God, Himself. Jesus quoted the Word and told him once again that He was God, and that "Him only shalt thou serve." Satan had no choice but to leave Him alone. Even though Satan has much power, his power could never equal that of Jesus. Everything concerning the betrayal of Jesus could not happen until He said it was going to. Judas was waiting for that green light from the lips of Jesus in order to betray the Lord. Until he got that go-ahead from Jesus, he knew that he could do nothing.

When Jesus finally gave Judas permission to betray Him[2], Satan then immediately entered into Judas to help him perform his mission. I want you to notice that everything was already set up perfectly so that it could happen quickly without anyone having the time to react to what was going on. In other words, Judas was working iniquity and setting things in place long before Jesus was ever betrayed. When you look at it in that context, it is amazing that the Antichrist cannot come on the scene until God gives him permission, and Jesus comes and pulls his born-again saints out of this world. The Bible is clear in II Thessalonians 2:3-7 that until He removes the Spirit of God out of this world, the Antichrist cannot come on the scene. However, the Bible says that as he waits, he is already working in the darkened shadows causing iniquity, murder, confusion, pain, and deception until the day God says, "It is time." God has already showed us through the life of Judas that the Antichrist must also wait for the time to be right until he is revealed to fulfill his task.

There is another truth about Judas that God wanted us to see concerning the events of his life. God, in his sovereign knowledge, gave us a vision of what is going to happen to the Antichrist in the Battle of Armageddon by example of the life of Judas. I believe that God is showing us that Judas and the Antichrist are the same throughout the entire Word of God. John 18:1-6 says that Judas gathered his band of soldiers, officers, and weapons in order to take Jesus. When Judas is enjoying his time in the spotlight, Jesus said unto them, "Whom seek ye?" It is a question to which they answered Him, "Jesus of Nazareth." All Jesus replied was, "I am He." The Bible said that as soon as He answered this, they all went backward and fell to the ground. Just the spoken Word of God was enough to slay his ene-mies in the blink of an eye. That is exactly what is going to happen to the Antichrist during Tribulation Period. Of all the different ways Jesus could destroy the Antichrist, He will do it by the Word of God in the Book of Revelations 19:15, 21. The Bible describes that just like Judas was a leader of an evil crowd that wanted Jesus dead, the Antichrist will also have a large multitude of people behind him. Instead of raining down fire from heaven and destroying him, Jesus has ordained destruction with the sword that proceedeth out of his mouth. Just like Judas and his crowd fell by the spoken Word, the Antichrist will also suffer the same fate in the battle of Armeggedon. It's phenomenal how Judas and the Antichrist seem to suffer the same demise.

The last thing that I want to bring to your attention is also very eye-opening, to say the least. Judas and the Antichrist are the only two me in the history of mankind that committed the worst sin known to man. They are forever guilty of betraying the innocent Blood of Jesus. In God's eyes, this is the worst sin ever committed among men. It is bad enough that Judas committed it in days gone by, but God is letting us know that the Antichrist will commit the same exact sin as he did in Matthew 27:4. Here he betrayed the Blood of Jesus, also. This is such an awful sin, that God will never forgive Judas for what he did to Jesus. Only a reprobate could betray someone that was so good to him. In the Tribulation Period, the Antichrist will also commit this horrible transgression found in Daniel chapter 11. It is called the Abomination of Desolation. The Antichrist will bring an unclean animal into the temple and sacrifice it on God's altar. When he does this, it will be an abomination to what Jesus did on the cross of Calvary where He shed His Blood for the sins of the world. This major sin will cause God to pour out judgement like this world has never seen. The Antichrist will betray the innocent Blood as well, and that will be the end of his spotlight, just as it was the end of Judas'.

I hope this quick little study helped you to realize how similar Judas and the Antichrist really are. As you get farther in this book, you will see how the comparison continues and the possibilities are

endless with these two men.

_____

[1] Mark 14:43
[2] John 13:27

THE MAN OF SIN

Our pastor, Timothy Ammon, is preaching through the book of Isaiah right know and while he was preaching he came to the characteristics of the Antichrist in Isaiah, chapters 9 and 10. He then turned over to Proverbs 6:15-19, showing us what the Antichrist will be like and what makes him who he is. The Antichrist is the total opposite of good and is the pure definition of evil. What's amazing about the seven deadly sins, stated in Proverbs 6:15-19, is that the Lord hates each one. These verses paint a scary picture of the Antichrist, who he is, and how he will carry himself. When the man of God was preaching, these verses opened up to me like never before. When reading these scriptures, I wrote the name 'Judas' in my Bible next to all seven, because I believe that nobody throughout the pages of the Bible (or history for that matter), fulfills these scriptures any more than Judas Iscariot. In the whole entire Bible you can never find Judas doing one thing to help or encourage Jesus. Everything Judas did was for himself. Judas was against God, causing only confusion and doubt among his fellow disciples. His deeds were always in secret and were for unholy or selfish motives. Judas was a devil from the beginning. He was double-minded, a thief, a liar, a murderer and a reprobate.

He performed his plan so well that he had everyone confused except Jesus. It's amazing that the Antichrist will have all the same characteristics that Judas did. As far as I can see in the Bible, there is not one single occurrence that Judas was ever under conviction to be saved. Judas, being a reprobate from his birth, proves to me that he was that "Man of Sin" which is described in II Thessalonians 2:3, referring to the Antichrist. It is clear in verse three that the Antichrist is given two titles from God for all eternity. One of these titles is the "Man of Sin," the other is the "Son of Perdition." Earlier I explained how Judas and the Antichrist are the only two people in the Bible that are called the Son of Perdition or Child of Hell. In Luke 22:53, when Judas betrays Jesus in the garden, he has a large group of people following him. Jesus was talking to Judas and his entire crowd, telling them that daily He clarified who he was and taught them in the temple. Never once did they stretch forth their hands against Him. Never did they try to take Him with swords and staves because, in Luke 22:22, it was determined that Judas would betray Jesus. The Lord said in verse 53 of that same chapter that this was their hour (notice the terminology), and the power of darkness referring to Judas or Satan. Many historians commonly call the Devil the "power of darkness." What is interesting about this statement is the fact that the only other place in the Bible that you will find this statement is in Colossians 1:13, were Paul is describing salvation.

The Bible says that when we accept Christ we are delivered from the power of darkness and are translated into God's kingdom. In other words, we go from Satan's side to Jesus Christ's side when we get saved. Once again, something to take note of, just as Judas and the Antichrist are called the Son of Perdition, Judas and the

Devil are given the title of "The Power of Darkness." This to me is very eye-opening because Jesus, Himself is making this statement about Judas; if Jesus makes a statement, you can take it to the bank. The Bible says, "Let God be true and every man a liar." Let me say that I am simply stating facts from the Bible and hardly any of this is my opinion. You don't have to believe me because I'm a sinner – but Jesus is the Way, the Truth, and the Life[1]. Also, heaven and earth shall pass away, but his word shall never pass away[2].

As I think about Judas and his life, there is not much said about this man. May I say that nearly everything said about his life is negative and evil. In Proverbs chapter 6, there are seven sins that are mentioned in that book and all of them are the major sins that God hates. Judas Iscariot did every one of these deadly sins in the few times he is mentioned in the pages of the Word of God. The fact that Judas did them so perfectly without anyone catching on, and that he did them in the very presence of the chosen few and Christ Himself, puts it over the top for me. Just as Satan could transform himself into an angel of light and deceive God's elect, Judas, that man of sin, could do the very same thing. I want you to notice these seven sins and show you how Judas lived these very sins that God talks about in Proverbs.

First of all, I want to show you that the first sin is a proud look. God hates pride or haughtiness. We see from the beginning of time that God cannot deal with pride or a proud look. The Lord proved that when He banished Satan and his following for trying to lift themselves above Jesus to ascend above God. That's what you call pride or being proud. The Bible says that the proud will be abased or brought low, and the humble will be exalted or uplifted. Just like Satan, the Antichrist will proclaim to be God and even sit in His temple. He will be filled with pride and will exhibit a proud look to all that gaze upon him. The Antichrist will have his thirty seconds of fame before Jesus will come and destroy all his works in the blink of an eye.

When we come to Judas, we find a man that was always haughty and self-motivated. Judas was evil or satanic from start to finish. Judas never helped Jesus; he only hurt Him. He stole from the Master, and never gave to anyone. Judas never one time humbled himself or asked Jesus any questions, because he was of a proud attitude. Judas lived such a deceitful and proud life that he had everyone fooled to what his true purpose was. Judas was the total opposite of Jesus. The Lord would always give, but Judas would always take. Jesus would humble Himself and Judas never would. Judas never one time displayed that he loved Jesus for what he did for him on a daily basis, but Jesus called him 'friend.' The fact is Judas wanted all the fame and glory that Jesus deserved. When Jesus had the woman pour out her year's wages at his feet it was a picture of what being humble really is. Jesus was enjoying her worship and he was receiveing all the glory, and Judas couldn't stand it, so he said in John 12:5, "Why was not this ointment sold, and given to the poor?" This only destroyed the moment and the praise that Jesus was getting. Jesus clarified that Judas could care less about the poor, but he was a thief and he bear what was in the bag. I want to say that Judas might have seemed right to the world, but God saw the pride of his heart and the sin of his proud look the whole time.

Secondly, I want to talk about his lying tongue for a moment. Judas Iscariot is no doubt the biggest liar that has ever lived. His whole life was based on trickery and deception. Everything Judas had wanted men to believe was lies. Jesus clarified that he was a devil for the entire three and half years, but every one else believed Judas to be good and a follower of Jesus. You will never find any of the chosen of God ever saying one bad thing about Judas (before his betrayal), but all the time he was a devil according to Jesus. That, my friends, is the very definition of a liar. The Bible declares that Satan is the 'father of lies' and that he is the master deceiver[3]. The Antichrist's rule and reign will be through lying and deceiving the people. Judas' life is no different and it was the true meaning of what being a liar is. At the Last Supper, Jesus plainly tells His disciples that Judas would betray Him. Judas had them so confused however, through his charisma and false appearance that they started to wonder if it was one of them that would betray Jesus (while in reality it was Judas the whole time).

Much like Satan and the Antichrist, Judas was and is on a mission to deceive as many as he can because he knows that his time is short. One day, all sin will be done away with, but as for now Satan will still use lies and false truths to deceive the world (just as Judas did).

The third sin that is described is no doubt the worst sin of all and is the most important in the mind of God. The most wicked sin known to man that has ever been committed is *hands that shed innocent blood.* We understand that Jesus died for the sins of the world and by doing so, shed his innocent blood for you and for me. Every man, woman, boy, or girl that has ever lived is responsible for shedding the blood of Jesus. There is one man, however, who was and always will be the chosen of God to betray the innocent blood of Jesus – that man is Judas Iscariot. Because he is the Man of Sin, he is the only man that was chosen to fulfil this horrible deed. The Bible is clear that his mission was to betray Jesus for thirty pieces of silver in Zechariah 11:12. He was the Son of Perdition, or the born-again of hell. He was the power of darkness or Satan, himself. It was determined or in the plan of God. Jesus declared that it was better that Judas would have never been born, speaking of future judgement. Judas went to his own place, referring to hell. I'm simply saying that his whole purpose or hour was to betray the innocent blood of Jesus.

You see, my friends, you can commit any sin that you desire and maybe get by with it, and God may forgive you. However if you blaspheme against the Holy Ghost or the Blood of Jesus, you will never be forgiven by God. The Bible says in Matthew 12:32 that when you cross this line you are as good as in hell, in the mind of God. Judas committed the worst sin, ever in the history of mankind, when he betrayed the most innocent blood of all – the Blood of Jesus.

The devil also betrayed Jesus in the beginning and paid the ultimate price. Much like Judas and the devil, the Antichrist follows the same exact pattern and also betrays the Blood of Jesus when he commits the Abomination of Desolation in the Tribulation Period. The fact that history repeats itself and that all three commit the same exact sin should prove to us that they are all of the same trinity. The Blood of Jesus is the most important thing in this universe, because without it we will all go to hell one day. With it, we can all go to heaven and dwell with God forever and ever. What Judas did was so vile and wicked in the mind of God, that he and he alone is the only man throughout history that could fulfil the title of, "The Man of Sin."

Therefore, Judas, the Antichrist and the Devil are one in the same. This title was given to Judas long before man was created, as a result of what Satan did at the start. The course of Satan's actions caused everything concerning Bible prophecy to already be determined in the ages to come. Jesus gave Judas this title before He was betrayed because He knew who would betray Him even before it was done. That is what jumps out to me about these seven sins the most. Judas, himself is responsible for betraying the very Blood of Jesus and causing the purity of God to be betrayed into the hands of sinners. Let me say that it doesn't get any worse than that.

The fourth sin that God hates is a heart that deviseth wicked imaginations. This sin is referring to somebody who is all the time thinking about wicked things, has evil imaginations, and a well thought-out plan to achieve their evil deeds. I think about when God destroyed the world with a flood back in Genesis simply because men's minds were only on evil continually. God designed men to think upon good and honest things[4], but when man begins to turn from God and their hearts grow dark, they have become evil in the sight of God. Judas had a plan that was executed perfectly. In other words, it was very well thought-out. It was very dark and very evil. His mind was extremely sharp and his actions were very private. His whole existence or goal was to devise wicked imaginations. He was an expert at his craft and his motive was to stay ahead of the game. He had the ability to get people to follow after his ideas and traps, and to side against Jesus. Judas had a blackened heart and was trying to steal the minds of everyone he could in his three and a half years of following Christ. Judas imagined how it would be one day to betray Jesus and be in the spotlight for a little while. When the time finally came, He was ready to take action and never stumbled in performing his task.

It was wicked imaginations that helped Judas fulfil his life-long goal and it will be no different for the Antichrist, as everything will be all thought-out, long before he comes on the scene. What the Bible teaches is that the coming of the Antichrist is *after* Satan with all power, signs, and lying wonders. What we are seeing in our day is the program that the Antichrist (or the mystery of iniquity) has already been setting-up to destroy the hearts of men. When I think of the hearts of men today it is only geared on perversion, sin, and lying wonders. When the Antichrist comes to rule this world, the minds and hearts of men will already be trained to his agenda. It will be simple for him to control the world because his plan is already being practiced by it. A good example is television, the Internet, and entertainment that has come on the scene in the last sixty years or so.

Sin is so easy to access in our day that you do not even have to leave your house anymore. It is global and sin is more common in our day than it has ever been in history – thanks to wicked imaginations. This plan has been spread throughout the whole world and it works right into the plan of Satan. The Devil knows exactly what he is doing because he walks about "seeking whom he may devour," and he is a lot smarter than you or me. I will prove to you that TV, Internet, and other avenues of technology have to be there in the Tribulation Period because that's how the Antichrist will be able to watch keep track of you. That was not possible sixty years ago, but it is now. Also, when God's two witnesses die in the Book of Revelations chapter 11, the Bible says that the whole earth will be watching because of technology. Just like Judas had wicked imaginations and had the world deceived, the Antichrist, through the wicked thoughts of men, will have everything set-up to rule and deceive. It is so easy to see if you just pay attention to what is going on.

The fifth sin that Jesus hates which Judas was guilty of is feet that are swift in running to mischief. This simply means that when good and evil presents itself, the evil man will be quick to choose the evil rather than the good. It means that when the time is right he will run to evil very quickly. Judas proved that what man sees on the outside doesn't always relate to what is on the inside. "Man looketh upon the outward appearance but God looketh on the heart." Judas proved that you cannot judge a book by its cover. The Bible teaches us that Judas' whole life was groomed for that one moment or chance to fulfil his goal. He seemed good for three and a half years, but the Bible says he sought opportunity to betray Him. Judas, much like the Antichrist, was waiting patiently in the shadows until that glad day when Jesus would give him the green light to fulfil his duty. It is at this moment that we truly see who he was the whole time. Judas did not argue with Jesus, he was just glad his time finally arrived. We see that through Judas' actions and how he sought opportunity to betray Him that he fulfils scripture. This proves that his feet were swift in running to mischief.

The Antichrist is no different. We know that after his time of peace is over, like Judas, his true colors will show and this world will be in for a rude awakening. When finally he has his chance, the Antichrist he will break the covenant that he had set-up and will become a monster that will fulfil his purpose to betray Jesus once again. It's amazing that all these sins are practiced by Judas as well as the Antichrist. That is the fifth sin.

When we get to the sixth sin that God hates, we find that it is similar to the second sin, which is a lying tongue. This sin, however, is referring to a false witness or preacher. Nobody is a more perfect example of a false preacher than Judas was. He has invented the modern day TV evangelist. Like I said earlier, Judas had more charisma and personality than any other preacher did in history, for he deceived the best of the best. He had the power to perform miracles and preach with authority, but his working was after Satan. Judas was a false teacher that brought in damnable heresies and the Bible says that many shall follow their pernicious ways. The Bible says that with feigned words they will make merchandise of you. In other words, they are in it for the money or other reasons besides preaching the truth. In Judas' case it was about money and power. Judas was very famous and seemingly powerful in his day, but was after Satan. The Bible teaches that every false witness will end up in chains of darkness when they die. It is amazing that in II Peter 2:4, God links up false teachers like Judas to the angels that sinned and were cast down into hell. Judas, no doubt, had these qualities and was truly the king of false teachers that God is warning us about. He was straight out of hell and his life proved it.

I can remember growing up at Van Born Baptist Church in Dearborn Heights, Michigan. This church, in my opinion, was one of the great churches of our generation. Van Born had about 90 members in that church and I remember one year they gave over two hundred thousand dollars to missionaries. This church was old-fashioned and had firm Bible believers. I remember when the Desert Storm War broke out and the war in Iraq raged on, people came knocking on the church door wanting to talk to the pastor about their souls. They were worried about the end of the world because members of that church knocked on doors from a five-mile radius from the church, warning people about hell and the Second Coming of Christ. We had a preacher come through Van Born Baptist Church that supposedly got saved out of the bars. This preacher came at a time when our preacher got sick and he could slip in. This man had an amazing musical talent and a good ability to preach. He had an incredible amount of charisma, as well.

He seemed like a perfect candidate to fill the gap caused by the pastor's sickness, but what we didn't know was that he was stealing money from certain members of the church while gaining the trust from the rest of the congregation. The entire time he was stealing from the church for his own personal gain. One of the greatest churches of our time has split and never truly recovered. My point in all of that was to show you that false teachers are different at home than they are in public.

Nobody was more of a false witness that spoke lies than this man named Judas. The Antichrist will also follow suit and be a false witness who deceives the world. He will preach and speak love, but his heart is full of evil. He will perform miracles but, in reality, he is forever lost. He will be about power and authority, and will care less who he hurts in the process. He will be the ultimate false witness, destroying millions in the process while fulfilling his unholy purpose. You see, Judas and the Antichrist are the kings of falsehood and lies. This proves the fact that Judas is a cut above any other false witness; in God's eyes, he is the Man of Sin.

There is one more sin that Judas committed on a regular basis to seal his fate as the Man of Sin. This sin is simply that of sowing discord among the brethren. The term "Devils Advocate" means, "a church official sent to find fault among the chosen few." Recall how Judas was the treasurer and that he fulfills this defination. Remember that the Son of Perdition is his title and Judas truly was that sort of person. Judas had a plan to keep confusion and discord among all that followed Jesus. He, in my opinion, always tried to keep the chosen of God guessing and fighting among themselves. When Jesus was enjoying the praise of Mary, because He had raised her brother Lazarus from the dead, Judas couldn't stand it. The offering of Mary was meant to honor Jesus like He had never been honored before – but instead, Judas (who was sent to cause discord or confusion among the brethren), stepped in. The Bible says that Judas stirred up the other disciples and caused them to murmur against Jesus and ruin His glory. In John 12:4, the Bible says that Judas questioned why the ointment was not given to the poor; In Matthew 26:8, the Bible says that the disciples had indignation or anger towards the woman, thanks to Judas.

Every time Jesus tried to show his disciples things or teach them, Judas was convincing them that Jesus was wrong. What's amazing is that in the Book of Acts, after Judas is dead and in his own place, the confusion is gone. Peter preaches and three thousand are saved. Judas completed all seven of these sins in his lifetime and he did it better than anyone who ever lived. It is common knowledge that the Antichrist is the most evil man ever to live and we have seen, so far, throughout this book that Judas clearly is that man that God chose. When looking at Judas and his life, it is very stunning how much his life parallels the Antichrist's and these seven sins that God hates in Proverbs 6: 16-19.

I want to close this point with the fact that in verse 15 the Bible teaches us that Judas (as well as the Antichrist), will fall into sudden destruction because of his sin, and will be broken without remedy.

You see, Judas and the Antichrist, no doubt, fit this description and their time is short to perform their unholy deeds. God will destroy them in a moment to fulfil scripture. I hope this has opened your eyes to Judas and the Antichrist like it has opened mine. Some things in the Word of God are undeniable and the life of Judas is one of them, AMEN.

---

[1] John 14:6
[2] Matthew 24:35
[3] John 8:44
[4] Philippians 4:8

HIS OWN PLACE

When I started studying the life of Judas Iscariot, I came across an amazing portion of scripture in the Bible. In Acts 1:25, the Holy Ghost wanted us to know something very clearly about Judas Iscariot. It's something I want to focus on very closely for a minute. Peter, led by the Holy Ghost, began to preach directly after the resurrection of Jesus Christ. The first thing that Peter wanted to express while speaking to the hundred and twenty in the upper room was that Judas was a devil from the very start. When you get to verse 25, the Holy Ghost plainly tells us that when Judas died he went "to his own place," referring to hell. This is extremely important when you start to break down the life of Judas.

When I think about what Jesus said about Judas, it is very alarming to say the least. Jesus, Himself labeled Judas as, "The Son of Perdition" in John 17:12. That title simply means, "child of damnation." What Jesus was saying is that Judas was familiar with this place called hell because that's where he's from. The Bible always means what it says and says what it means. In Acts 1:25, when the Bible said that Judas went to his own place, that is exactly what it means and I will prove it to you. I want to show you something that God gave me one day at work that will totally shock you and prove the fact that Judas' home has and always will be hell. The Word of God is clear in Matthew 25:41 that hell was not created for mankind in its original design, but was created long before man ever existed. Hell was created or prepared directly as a result of what Satan did at the beginning of time, when he and his following rebelled against God. Satan desired to elevate or lift himself above God and tried to take His throne in Isaiah 14:12-15 and II Peter 2:4. When that moment in time occurred, God had no other choice than to prepare a place called hell – designed for the devil and his angels, according to Matthew 25:41. In other words, hell itself was not created for man but rather for the devil and his angels. What makes this so interesting concerning Judas is that when he died, the Bible says he went to his own place. The question I have for you is simple. If Judas was a normal man like you and me, and hell was not prepared for us, then how could Judas go to his own place if he was a normal man? Judas would have to be a devil or one of his angels for him to fulfil that scripture. I say to you that Judas is the Antichrist, which is why the Bible says he went to his own place!

Another verse of scripture that supports this thought is found in Proverbs 9:18. The Bible is clear that when a man dies without Jesus Christ, God has no other choice than to put them in hell. Proverbs declares that mankind is a guest in the blackened pits of the damned. In other words, they have never been there before and are only guests to hell, while Satan and his angels alone are the proud owners because it was made for them. Think about it – if Judas were a normal man like you and me, then wouldn't he have only been a guest when he got to hell? The Holy Ghost wanted us to know that when this man died, he went to his own place. God was letting us know that this was not Judas' first time arriving in hell but rather this was his home, or his own place.

I often think about my own place and how familiar I am becoming with the concept that I have my own place now. The simple fact of the matter is if I wanted to invite people over to my house for any reason and they decided to accept my invitation to come, they would be my invited guests. Because I own my house, the people that decided to come would simply be my guests and I would be their host. When Judas died and went to hell, he should have only been a guest (just like any other lost soul), but he was more than just a man; he was the Son of Perdition and the Man of Sin. These verses of scripture alone should really open your eyes to the reality of who Judas is. The Bible is clear that Judas was not of this world but was born right out of the pit of hell, thus fulfilling his title of the Son of Perdition. Ignore the opinion of man or what you have been taught your whole life – if it does not line up with the Bible, then it is wrong. Remember that if Judas was a man like you or me, and hell was not created for man, then he could not go to his own place! Judas was a devil and the Bible plainly expresses that. You cannot be a guest and an owner at the same time. That is also something to think about. Judas was either a guest of hell or it was his own place. So by that conclusion alone, we see that hell was his own place and that he was not of this world. I sure hope this simple Bible truth helped you to understand Judas Iscariot a little better.

I want to clarify one thing about hell. We that understand the Bible are aware of the fact that, much like everything else, God is the true owner of hell. We know that he created it and has the keys to it in Revelation 1:18, but that doesn't change the fact that it was prepared as a result of what the devil did in the beginning by sinning against God. Just like God has a home, the Devil has a home. Hell was designed by God, Himself as a holding place for sin in general. From the time the Devil fell, he has been paying for his sin ever since.

Those that have bought a home and still owe money on it under-stand that it is their place as long as they continue to make payments every month. If we ever stop making our payments then our home will no longer be ours. As long as we continue paying those costs on our home, it is considered ours and we are the owners of it. If you don't believe that, then don't pay your house payment next month and we will see who really owns it. God is in control of this situation and He has the Devil on a never-ending payment plan. The only way that hell will cease to be the Devil's home is if he stops paying for it. The good news is that Satan will always have to pay for what he did to God at the beginning of time and God will always make sure that payments continue to come in.

God the Father has the Devil in bondage to Him and even though he will never be able to claim hell as his own, that doesn't change the fact that it was made for him. He will always have to call hell his home, whether he wants to or not. As long as he keeps making payments it will continue to be his home, or the place in which he dwells, for all eternity. Therefore, God's home will always be heaven and the Devil's home will always be hell. I just wanted to explain when I said that the Devil and his demons owned it, that it was simply their home because they have never stopped paying for it and never will. God owns everything and He is renting the Devils home to him, whether he wants to or not.

MY FAMILIAR FRIEND

Something that I feel is pretty amazing when you really think about it is a verse of scripture found in Psalms 41:9. It is in that verse of scripture that the Bible calls Judas a familiar friend to Jesus. The word "familiar" simply means 'to be closely acquainted with or to have previous encounters with.' In other words, each person will know each other very well. If you have never met somebody before, it would be impossible to be familiar with that person without having had any previous history with them. What is amazing about this verse of scripture is the fact that David, led of the Holy Ghost, wrote this scripture around one thousand years before Judas or Jesus were ever born in the New Testament. My question to you would have to be, "How were Jesus and Judas already familiar with each other if their births had not yet taken place?"

I remember when I first met my wife. I started visiting a church called Hope Baptist Church. My full intention was to only hear the preaching of the Word of God and nothing else. I went for a couple of weeks and, to this point, I had never met my wife or knew anything of her yet. We finally met and started going on dates together because we wanted to become familiar with each other. The more times we went out together, the more we started to learn about each other, or became familiar with one another. After many dates and experiences of getting to know one another, she has become my familiar friend. May I say this would have been impossible before my visit to Hope Baptist Church because we had never met, up to that point.

What the Bible is teaching us in this verse is that long before Jesus and Judas ever met in the New Testament, they had already become familiar with each other prior their physical birth. That's why David wrote that verse one thousand years before Judas was born in the Book of Psalms. No one is more familiar with Jesus than Satan, for they met on a daily basis. Because Judas is the Antichrist and part of the unholy trinity, the Lord is more familiar with him than any other person on earth. God created Satan in the beginning, and wanted him to be his friend, worshipping Him forever. When Satan rebelled, he went from God's friend to his familiar friend in a moment. God and Satan are in contact on a daily basis because he is the accuser of the brethren and, in Job chapter 1, we find him appearing before God in the life of Job. Also, he walks to and fro in the earth, seeking whom he may devour[1]. Night and Day, Satan and God are engaged in a spiritual battle that will never end until Satan is put in hell at the Great White Throne Judgment, which is found in Revelation 20: 11-15.

God was showing us in Psalms 41:9 that, long before their ministries began during the life of Jesus Christ, the battle had started at the beginning of time. Judas could not be familiar with Jesus before their births if they had not had previous encounters long before.

I also think that it is very interesting that Jesus said the following in Matthew 26:50 concerning Judas as he came to betray Him: "Friend wherefore art thou come?" Judas had never been a friend to Jesus one time in his life, yet He called him His friend. In the Proverbs 17:17, we see what a true friend really is. In that verse, the Bible says that a friend loveth at all times. Even though Jesus was always good to Judas (despite the fact that he knew he would betray Him one day), Judas never fulfilled the definition of a friend. So the question is, "Why did Jesus call him His friend if He knew that Judas had just betrayed Him?" Just as we already discussed about Judas being His familiar friend or someone He had met before, Jesus wanted the world to know that even though Judas hated Him, the Lord still loved Judas and treated him well – no matter what was done to Him. Think about it… If you have a true friend, the Bible says that he will love at all times and always be there for you. In other words, you will both love each other mutually. If they were so close, then why did Judas seek to betray Jesus? That goes against the Bible and the true meaning of a friendship between two parties. Who really was the friend in this situation between Judas and Jesus? The answer is Jesus. He still considers the Devil a familiar friend, or someone that He was so good to in His life. You could think of Jesus and Judas as being familiar with one another because they have known each other since the beginning of time. Their days of battle are long from over and they will always be enemies, or familiar friends, until the end of time. I hope this simple thought helped you to understand why Jesus and Judas were familiar with each other before they appeared in their earthly ministries.

Another thing that is worth noting about Psalms 41:9 is that out of any man that God could have chosen to pen these words down in the Bible, it is none other than King David. Are you aware of the fact that out of all the thrones that God could have chosen to sit upon during the Millennial Reign, He chose that of King David's[2]? We understand that before Jesus has a chance to sit upon David's throne in the Millennial Reign, the Antichrist will claim to be God and sit down upon the throne, blaspheming the Holy Ghost. That's when Jesus will descend from heaven to destroy the Antichrist at the Battle of Armageddon and reclaim His rightful place on David's throne. The Lord Jesus will once again meet his familiar friend in the Valley of Megiddo and will slay him with the sword that proceedeth out of his mouth.

So the days of battle for these two adversaries are still to come when they meet in the battle of all battles. With that being said, there was a reason that God choose David to write this verse. It shows us that the days of Jesus and Judas are not over. These familiar friends will, no doubt, meet again at the end of the Tribulation Period. It is no wonder why Jesus said in Matthew 26:24, "Woe unto that man by whom the Son of Man is betrayed! It had been good for that man if he had not been born." Jesus knew all things that would take place and He was saying in that verse that He will meet Judas again in the future and this time He will get His revenge. He will destroy the Antichrist in front of the whole world.

Another thing that is interesting about the terminology of familiar friend is the fact that, in the Old Testament, God often talked about people that had familiar spirits. God always linked people that had familiar spirits together with demonic spirits. All throughout the Old Testament you will find people that had familiar spirits seeking out others that had the same type of spirit. Psalms 41:9 is an Old Testament scripture and, everywhere else previous to this verse, the term "familiar" is always referring to demons. For example, in I Samuel 28: 7-9, Saul was battling with his own personal demons and wanted answers. The Bible says that Saul sought out familiar spirits and took his problems to none other than a witch. God had refused to speak to Saul anymore, so he had no other choice than to seek familiar spirits (someone that had the same problem as he). All throughout the Old Testament, God compared familiar spirits to demons.

If you consider Psalms 41:9, why did Jesus call Judas His familiar friend, when He could have just called him His friend? We can see that God is simply linking the life of Judas to that of demonology or familiar spirits. When Jesus came on the scene, demon activity was at an all time high. It seemed like everywhere Jesus or Judas went that demons were present. Jesus is the one that called Judas a devil, not me. He is the one that gave Judas the title, "Son of Predition," not me. Jesus is the one who said that he was the power of darkness, not me. So you see that Jesus was telling us in Psalms 41:9 that the life of Judas Iscariot is just like all the other examples of people with familiar spirits in the Old Testament. Judas' spirit can and always will be the same as demons. Wherever Judas Iscariot went demons or evil spirits were nearby.

---

[1] I Peter 5:8
[2] Luke 1:32

WHY DOES JUDAS APPEAR IN
THE OLD TESTAMENT?

When I began to study the life of Judas Iscariot, I looked at the obvious or common things relating to him, but I found very little was said. Therefore I had to look deep into the Scriptures to find certain aspects about Judas Iscariot. One of the most interesting things about this man Judas is the fact that he is the only lost man ever to be prophesied in the Old Testament that appears in the New Testament. This is very important simply because of the fact that an Old Testament prophet had to be exactly right when he made a prediction or he wouldn't be considered a true prophet. If his prediction was wrong He would be taken out and stoned to death for being a false prophet. Zechariah predicted that Judas was going to betray the Lord for thirty pieces of silver hundreds of years later and, because he was a prophet, it had to happen exactly like he said. If it had not, the Bible would be broken and false. However, we understand that Judas did indeed betray Jesus for thirty pieces of silver, just like Zechariah said way back in the Old Testament. In other words, when the Bible said Judas would betray Jesus, it had to take place just as it said.

David, in the Book of Psalms, made the same prediction hundreds of years before Zechariah did, and we know that he was right as well. Every prophecy written in the Bible has taken place or will take place in the future, or the Bible would be false. We that understand the scriptures know this from Psalms 119:89. That Scripture says that God's Word is settled in heaven; Matthew 24:35 states that heaven and earth shall pass away, but his words will never pass away. The simple fact is the Bible has no errors and if the Bible says it, mark it down – it is settled.

Everything concerning Bible prophecy is already determined in the mind of God. For example, everything that the Old Testament prophets said about the birth, death, trial, betrayal, and Resurrection of Jesus had to happen in the New Testament exactly like it was described or the Bible would be false. The good news is all the prophecies concerning Jesus came true. This proves the Old Testament. All the prophecies concerning John the Baptist had to come true as well, or the Bible would have errors. We understand that the forerunner came and it once again fulfilled scripture. What's shocking is that Judas, a lost man, is prophesied to one day fulfil his lifelong mission and betray Jesus. We know that he did fulfill the scripture.

There is no place in the entire Bible where Judas is ever under conviction and this explains why. Consider the following: if Judas would have ever been under conviction and got saved, then the Scriptures would have been broken, causing all the scriptures that proclaimed his betrayal of Jesus to be a lie. Jesus also told His disciples that Judas was a devil in John 6:70 and that the scriptures couldn't be broken. He called him the Son of Perdition, which means the child of hell. We know that if Jesus made a statement, it is true for all time because He is incapable of lying or sinning[1]. Jesus clearly knew that Judas would betray Him before it happened because He is God. He knew that Judas was lost because He is sovereign and you will never once find where God invited Judas or smote him with conviction to get saved. Where do you find Judas seeking Jesus or asking Him to be saved?

There was an understanding that scripture was already in place and, in the foreknowledge of God, Judas had to betray Jesus in order to fulfill scripture. Judas had a different motive than the other disciples; he did not want to help Jesus, but only to hurt Him. Judas never asked any questions the way the other eleven always did. It seemed like Judas and Jesus always knew the next step and had an understanding between the two of them. Judas was always at the right place, at the right time, and was always ready to fulfill prophecy. If Judas were like you and me, there would definitely be a time in the Bible where he was at least under conviction while following Jesus. The fact is that he was not there to be saved; he was there to betray Jesus and fulfill scripture.

There is another thing concerning Judas in the Old Testament that is also worth noting. In the Book of Zechariah chapter 11, Judas appears hundreds of years before his birth. What's amazing about this is that the whole chapter is talking about what the Antichrist will do in the future. It discuss the time when he will break the covenant that he had set-up between Judah and Israel at the start of the Tribulation Period. Then, all of a sudden, Judas starts talking hundreds of years before his birth. This relates to the fact that, just like he betrayed the Lord for thirty pieces of silver, he will break his covenant that he had made with all the people. So, in other words, Judas is telling us in the future that he will fulfill the title that Jesus gave him as the Son of Perdition. Why in the world would Judas appear in the same chapter as the Antichrist before either of their existences began? There is more to this man named Judas than meets the eye.

You will find that Judas is very similar to the Antichrist when you study it, though little is written about him. I want you to read Zechariah chapter 11 and tell me what you read. You will find that without switching characters, Judas and the Antichrist are indeed the same person. I feel that it is very interesting how Judas appears in the Old Testament, for the simple fact that all which is written of him is in a future tense or prophecy. If a man dies lost, according to the Bible, he has no future except a life in hell and an existence without God. Judas is more than just a man; he is the Antichrist. Just like he fulfilled the Old Testament already, he will also fulfil the New Testament and become the Son of Perdition, right before your very eyes. If you read John 17:11 and II Thessalonians 2:3, you will find that Judas and the Antichrist are the same person, just as Zechariah teaches us.

We have seen in this chapter that prophecy must be fulfilled exactly like it is written or it would cease to be prophesy. All throughout the Bible, we understand that prophecy came true exactly the way in which it was written. I want to conclude this chapter with the simple truth that in the life of Judas it is no different. We find in Acts 1:16 how Judas fulfilled the mission that was declared of him way back in Psalms 41:9 (according to Peter as he preached on the day of Pentecost, in the upper room). It is there in that verse of scripture that Peter, filled with the Holy Ghost, announced to the entire world that what Judas had done (just a few days earlier) fulfilled Psalms 41:9. The Bible says in Acts 1:16 that this scripture must needs have been fulfilled concerning Judas. What Peter was clearly saying is that, in betraying the Lord, Judas completed the mission to fulfill his prophecy.

The fact that it was already prophesied a thousand years earlier should not have been a surprise to anyone, but rather should have been a fulfillment of scripture. What Peter was telling the people is that Judas had to betray the Lord because that's what he was sent to do, as clearly expressed by Acts 1:16. So you see, Judas' betraying of the Lord proves the Bible once again; and truely reveals to us that this was his purpose the entire time, according to the Bible. I will simply say that if you don't believe me, it is all right. However, it is hard to argue with the Word of God when it speaks of Bible prophecy and this man named Judas.

---

[1] II Corinthians 5:21

10 MAJOR REASONS THAT JUDAS WAS SATAN'S SON

J ust like Jesus was God's only Begotten Son and manifested Himself among men, the Bible teaches that Judas was Satan's son, and He also manifested himself among those same men. Earlier I said that everything God originates, the Devil imitates; it is no different in this situation. The Devil knew that Jesus, God in the flesh, was sent to be the Savior of the world, and to rescue this earth from hell. The Devil has had one goal since the beginning of time and that is to do everything in his power to stop Jesus from making it to the cross. If he could stop the Lord from succeeding, then he could cause Him to sin, and we would be on are way to hell. Thank God, Jesus was perfect and the Devil failed. Satan knew that he had to have the best of the best for this important job, so he sent *his* son to try to stop Jesus.

The Bible teaches us that the Devil clearly has a son, just like God has a Son. In Genesis 3:15 it is clear that Satan would have a cursed seed who would appear on earth one day as the Devil's son, and would walk during the time of Christ. If you will read verse 14 of this chapter you will find that, as a result of sin entering the world through Satan beguiling Eve, God cursed the woman's seed (as well as that of the Devil's). We understand that every person that is born in this world through the womb of a woman is a sinner because of the sin of Eve. The Bible is clear in Genesis 3:20 that Adam called his wife Eve, which means the mother of all living. Because of Eve's disobedience in the Garden of Eden, all of her seed must carry the curse of sin as long as people are born. God cursed the seed of the woman because she went against the plan of God.

On the other hand, there was also a curse that God placed on the Devil's seed. The Bible is clear that just like God had a Son, the Devil will also have a son. The Book of Genesis 3:15 states that he will be "cursed from his foundation." The Bible says that "God will put enmity between thee and the woman." The word enmity means warfare. In other words, God has shown us in this verse that the Devil's son will have war in his heart and forever fight against all mankind. The Bible is teaching us in the Book of Genesis that Satan indeed has a seed that has and will continue to fight against Christ. In this verse, when God is talking about the seed of Satan, He also refers to the Seed of the woman – the Lord Jesus Christ. The Bible tells us (thousands of years before Christ walked on planet earth) that Satan and his seed, Judas, would bruise His heel on the cross; God, in contrast, would bruise his head when He rose from the dead.

We clearly see the two trinities at work as early as Genesis 3:15. The word, 'seed' simply means a by-product of your father and mother, or an offspring. The simple fact is the Devil has a son and his name is Judas, according to the Word of God. The Devil imitated what God originated in the life of Judas Iscariot. When God robed His Son in flesh (through the womb of a woman) to die for the sins of the world, Satan knew he had to match Him the best way he could.

Therefore, as a result, he wrapped his son in human flesh in the form of Judas Iscariot. Let's stop and think about this for a second. If you were to study the life of Judas Iscariot in great detail, you would discover that this man was more responsible for Jesus dying on the cross than any other human in history. The angry counsel, along with the Jewish race, could not have achieved what they did without the help of Judas. The Devil's son was the mediator, or the go between, that this world needed in order to crucify Jesus. Without the help of Judas, this world could have never crucified the Lord.

When I think about this Bible truth, it immediately brings my mind back to Genesis chapter 3, verse 15. In the plan of God, Satan's son was the only possible man who could betray the Lord and cause his heel to be bruised on the cross. This man's life was demonic from the start and, throughout the Scriptures, we can see it. I want to quickly say once again when it comes to the Bible that I didn't write it, but only recite it. If you have a disagreement with what is in this book, then please take it up with God; not me! When Judas Iscariot betrayed Jesus in the Garden of Gethsemane, he fulfilled Genesis chapter 3:15 in the process.

I will give you many different reasons why I believe that Judas Iscariot was the very son of the Devil, himself. I want you to judge these reasons and consider who this man is.

1. One of the major reasons I believe that Judas was Satan's son is because Jesus, Himself (in John 17:12), called him the Son of Perdition. The term, "Son of Perdition," is defined as "child of hell or damnation." Notice the terminology 'Son of Perdition' and 'Child of Hell.' This term is only found in one other place in the entire Bible and it is II Thessalonians 2:3 when describing the Antichrist. If they were different people, then God would have called them the *sons* of perdition because they were two separate people. Rather, God called them the *Son* of Perdition – proving that they were one and the same. I looked up the word "son" in Webster's Dictionary and it is defined as a male in relation to his parents. Judas was the Devil's only son, and the Bible is clear about that. Jesus called Judas "The Son of Perdition," even before he actually betrayed Him. Jesus was letting us know in John chapter 17 (when he prayed in the Garden of Gethsemane), that He and the Father had already labeled Judas Iscariot as the child of the Devil. This was given long before he betrayed Him in His earthly ministry, and a result of what he did at the beginning of time. When you study your Bible, it is clear that Judas and the Antichrist are the only two men with this description, because they are the same person. That's why Jesus said Judas was a Devil; He knew all things, including what would happen next. The Son of Perdition is singular – Judas Iscariot or the Man of Sin. It really makes perfect sense.

2. Another major reason that I strongly believe the Devil's son was Judas is because of what Jesus said about him in Luke 22:53. It is the well-known chapter where the Lord is betrayed in the garden. The Bible speaks of how Judas came immediately after Jesus said he would, and it is there where Jesus clarified that never once as He taught daily in the temple did they ever try to take Him by force, with staves, or with swords. In other words, without the approval of Jesus, they could do nothing. However, the Lord wanted the world to know that this was their hour (referring to people that were following Judas). The Bible follows by saying, "…and the power of darkness," referring to Judas. We understand clearly that Jesus is directly speaking to him because all of the Old Testament scriptures talk only of the hour in which Judas would betray Jesus – in other words, this was his destiny. What is interesting about the statement, "the Power of Darkness," is that just like the Son of Perdition is only found twice in the Bible (referring to the same person), the phrase "the Power of Darkness" is no different. It is found one time in the Book of Luke when Jesus called Judas the 'Power of Darkness,' and it is found a second time in Colossians 1:13, when it is referring to the Devil. The Bible is explaining salvation in that verse and expressing how before we are saved, we are controlled by the Devil or the Power of Darkness. When we get saved, we are translated from darkness into the kingdom of His Dear Son, referring to Jesus. Those are the only two times that the Power of Darkness is used in the Bible, and we can see that it is referring to the same person. It is common knowledge that the Devil is called the Power of Darkness by many. Isn't it strange that when Jesus wanted to describe Judas in the garden, He used the same phrase as that of the Devil in the Book of Colossians?

3. The third reason as to why I am convinced that Judas was the Devil's son is the fact that only once in the Bible is a man referred to as the Devil or a devil. Once again, we see this pattern with Satan and Judas. We know that in the Book of Matthew chapter 4 he clarifies how Satan, himself was tempting and battling Jesus for forty days and nights. Other than this one instance when Jesus clarifies that this is the Devil, there is nowhere else that God describes somebody as the Devil or a Devil – except this man named Judas Iscariot. In John 6:70, Jesus confesses to the twelve disciples that one of them is a Devil and He was speaking to none other than Judas Iscariot, himself.

4. The fourth reason that I believe that Judas was the Devil, manifested in the flesh, is because when he died (Acts 1:25), the Word is clear that Judas went to his own place, speaking of hell. As we have talked about already in Matthew 25:41, hell was not created for mankind in it's origination, but rather for the Devil and his angels long before man was created. When men die without God and go to hell[1], they are only guests in the pit because it is their first time and because it is reserved for the devil and his angels. If Judas was a normal man, he would be only a guest in hell and it would not be his own place, like the Bible says. You cannot be a guest and an owner of a place at the same time. If hell was his own place, then that makes him the Devil or one of his angels because the Scripture must be fulfilled. When the Bible said he went to his own place that is exactly what it means. As we have seen with the first three points of this study, Judas and the Devil are the same person and part of the unholy trinity. Just like we have our own home, and have been there before, and are familiar with it, the same applies to hell being Judas' home. The Bible is teaching us that Judas was formed right out of hell, like the Antichrist is, and that's why he went to his own place.

5. This fifth reason will really start to open it up and prove to you that Judas was indeed the Devil's son. If you will search the four gospels of the New Testament and study the life of Judas and Jesus, you will never find one time where Judas was ever under conviction to be saved. Although Jesus knew that he was lost the whole time, He never dealt with or invited Judas to come to Him, nor will you find Judas having a desire to accept Him as his Savior. There are major reasons for this and I will explain them to you. The Bible is clear that Jesus came to seek and to save that which was lost. Having tasted death for every man, He is not willing that any should perish, but that all should come to repentance. Jesus died for the sins of the world, and invites anybody to come to Him to be saved. However, in the case of this man, we find that Judas is the only one throughout the history of the world that God refused to deal with or convict during his lifetime. I will explain why right know. In Matthew 12:31-32 and Mark 3:29, we find the sin of blaspheming the Holy Ghost. Jesus is clear when a man or woman steps over that line and commits this sin that it is the only sin in which he or she can never be forgiven for in this world or the world to come. Also, in Mark 3:29 it says that you are in danger of eternal damnation. What the Bible is teaching us in these verses is that a man or woman can commit any sin and be forgiven for it. However, if a man blasphemes the Holy Ghost they have eternally crossed that line and are a reprobate in the mind of God. In His mind, they are as good as in hell and God is done fooling with them forever. When Judas committed this sin in the beginning of time, he became a reprobate. When a man becomes a reprobate, the Bible[2] says that he gives them up to a reprobate mind. When God gives a man up to a reprobate mind, He is forever done convicting that man or woman and, in the heart of God, they are bound for hell. We have seen that Judas and the Devil are one and, because of that fact, it is understood why Jesus never invited Judas to come to Him for salvation in His earthly ministry.

Judas was a reprobate long before he followed Jesus, because he, being the devil's son, blasphemed the Holy Ghost in the beginning of time, as found in Isaiah 14:10-14 and also II Peter 2:4. This is one major reason why Judas was never under conviction during the earthly ministry of Jesus, because he was guilty of blaspheming the Holy Ghost; once this occurs, there is no forgiveness in this world or the world to come. The Bible tells us that Judas is the only man that God never dealt with because he was in the unholy trinity and because he blasphemed the Holy Ghost long before he appeared on earth.

Another reason he was a reprobate and you can never find God dealing with him is because of the Old Testament Scriptures concerning Judas. \When an Old Testament prophet made a prediction, he had to be exactly right or they would take him out in the street and stone him to death for being a false prophet. That's what made them a Bible prophet – they had to be exactly right in their prophecy, or the Bible would be false. We know that Judas fulfilled these prophecies of betraying Jesus because the Bible is perfect. Judas had to betray Him in order to fulfill the Scriptures concerning him. If Judas would have been under conviction to be saved in the Bible, then that would have broken the Scriptures concerning him. That's why Jesus never convicted him about his soul. If He would have dealt with him, it would go against other scripture already established about him in the Old Testament. That's why Judas was sent to this earth – to simply fulfill the Scriptures that were written of him.

Jesus, Himself would often tell His disciples that Judas was going to betray Him as well. If Jesus makes a statement it will be true from that time until forever because He is God. Jesus never invited him to get saved because He knew all things concerning the Scriptures, because He was God. If Jesus said Judas was going to betray him, He would be contradicting Himself if He would have dealt with him about his soul. The Book of James tells us that "a double-minded man is unstable in all his ways." There is no way that God would ever go against what He has already written in His Word. Those are the main reasons why you will never find Judas seeking to be saved, because he was a reprobate and he had to fulfill what was written of him in the Old and New Testaments.

6. Another reason Judas is the Devil's son would have to be the fact that when it came time to betray Jesus, it says in Luke 22:3 that Satan, himself entered into him to complete his lifelong mission. Just like Judas is the only man recorded in the Bible to go to his own place, Judas is the only man that ever had Satan, himself enter into him. You will often find demon-possessed men throughout the

Bible[3], and also Satan filling people's hearts and minds with evil thoughts or actions[4]. In contrast, never in the Bible has the Devil, himself entered into one single man – except one (you guessed it); Judas Iscariot. Judas is the Son of Perdition or the born-again of hell. In the Tribulation Period there will be another time in which Satan has entered into a man, and it is the Antichrist. Isn't it amazing that the only two men that Satan, himself entered into were Judas and the Antichrist?

7. Something else that is staggering about Judas Iscariot is the fact that he is the only lost man ever to be prophesied in the Old Testament that appears in the New Testament. If my count is correct, this is only true of three men. One of them is of course the Son of God who was proclaimed to be the Savior of the world, and that is exactly what He is. Another is John the Baptist, who was proclaimed to be the forerunner and preparer of the way of Jesus. John fulfilled all of the prophesies that were written of him. Both of these men were obviously saved and they were always in the plan of God. We understand Jesus was God manifested in the flesh, so I can see why he would appear in the Old Testament. John the Baptist was his fore-runner, or one that prepared the way for Jesus, so I can also see why God would proclaim him in the Old Testament.

When it comes to Judas, however, he is also prophesied in the Old Testament, but as the great traitor (one who will betray Jesus). The fact that God would proclaim Judas' arrival long before he actually showed up is worth taking note of. Just like Judas was a pre-determined man, the Antichrist is also pre-determined in the mind of God. Why would Jesus choose Judas, out of all the people in the world, to betray Him in the future? Judas even speaks out in Zechariah 11:10-13 about how he was going to betray the Lord for thirty pieces of silver and relates that to how he is going to break his covenant with all people during the Tribulation Period. If Judas was just a man, how in the world does he know what he is going to do in the future when he is not even born yet? Also, why is he talking as the Antichrist in Zechariah chapter 11 when he wouldn't be born until hundreds of years later? That would be an impossibility. That's why Judas is the Antichrist, for long before he was born in the flesh, his future was already determined as the Son of Perdition.

8. The names that the Bible uses to describe Judas Iscariot fit the description of the Devil or his son. For example, the word Judas itself means "traitor or one who betrays another." In Luke 6:16 we found that the Bible calls Judas the traitor. If you will read the Book of Psalms chapter 55, it relates the fact that Judas lived a life of deceit and deception. The Bible expresses that just like Judas was a traitor from the start, the Antichrist will also be a traitor and will break his covenant with the people that trusted in him. Once again we find Judas and the Antichrist being compared to one another. In the same chapter of Psalms 55:20-23 we can find that the words that the Antichrist will speak will be "smoother than butter, but war is in his heart: his words will be softer that oil, yet were they drawn swords." In other words, what is coming out of his mouth does not match up with what is in his heart. That is exactly the description of Judas in his earthly ministry. If you read verse number twenty-three, the Bible clarifies that men that have lived this lifestyle shall be brought down into the pit of destruction, and bloody and deceitful men shall not live out half of their days. It's amazing that Judas also fulfilled this Scripture as well. We understand that Judas died at an early age when he hung himself in the Book of Acts. It's stunning that not once, but twice, Judas and the Antichrist appear in the same chapters of two different books of the Old Testament. If Judas was just a man, then why is he always compared to the Antichrist? Judas definitely fulfills this title of a traitor, as does the Antichrist.

Are you aware of the fact that the term "Devil's advocate" simply means a church official that is assigned to find fault with those selected for beatification? Think about how Judas was a church official, or part of the Lord's twelve-member congregation. Jesus chose him to be treasurer of all the funds that came in during His three and a half year earthly ministry. Jesus chose him even though He clarified that he was a thief in John 12:6. Maybe Jesus chose him to fulfill his title. Also found in the same chapter, we see his other description fulfilled when it comes to being the Devil's advocate. He is assigned to find fault with those selected, cause them confusion, or to stir up the chosen. When the woman in John chapter 12 gave of her years' wages to magnify the Savior, the Bible is clear that Judas was responsible of stirring up the other disciples and causing them to murmur against Jesus. The term "Devil's advocate" has a definition that matches Judas very well.

We understand that Jesus clearly called Judas a Devil in John 6:70. It is interesting that Jesus choose to use this terminology. The term 'Devil' is defined as a wicked person with an evil spirit, often a child who is mischievous. We fully know that Judas was a wicked man on the inside. Very few times in the entire Bible is Judas ever referred to other than in a negative sense. The only time in which anything at all was said well of Judas was in Psalms 55:12-14. Every other time Judas is mentioned in the Word of God is in a negative way. Judas, no doubt, had an evil spirit about him, for he is the very man that betrayed the Son of God. We clearly see why Jesus called Judas a Devil, because he almost always fulfilled this description.

The fourth term that I want to examine when describing Judas is one we already covered. It is the term Son of Perdition. We understand that Judas and the Antichrist are the only two men in the Bible that are named this. The Son of Perdition simply means "child of hell or damnation." When the Bible says in the Book of Acts chapter 1 that Judas went to his own place, we clearly see how he is the Son of Perdition. His very existence was formed straight from the bellies of hell. Much like the Antichrist, everything concerning Judas was already determined before he ever walked upon earth. Their plan is devised right out of hell and nothing will ever change it. Jesus called Judas the Son of Perdition in John 17:12 to connect the dots and to show us that Judas and the Antichrist is truly the same person.

The last term I want to look at concerning Judas Iscariot is the term "Power of Darkness." We that understand the Bible and spiritual things fully comprehend that this is referring to the Devil, himself. In the Book of Luke 22:53, Jesus calls Judas the 'Power of Darkness.' In Colossians 1:13, the Bible refers to Satan as the 'Power of Darkness' as well. What Jesus was letting us know when he called Judas the Power of Darkness is that the Devil, himself was helping him complete his goal of betraying the Son of God (as they are, in essence, the same). 'Power of Darkness' means "pure evil," or having the authority to perform evil. We all understand that the Devil was the Power of Darkness, but the thing we all should consider is why was Judas called the very same thing.

When I think about these five descriptions of Judas, it is remarkable that Jesus is making at least half of them. In describing these few definitions we can see that most of the phrases involving Judas and who he was compare him to a child, or a son. There are many other phrases, quotes, and verses that speak in a negative way about him, but these are the five that really stuck out to me. When you look at these handfuls of definitions concerning Judas Iscariot and you start adding things up, you will begin to be convinced; much like I now am.

Oliver B. Green, the famous and great man of God from years ago, was quoted as saying, "When it comes to Judas Iscariot, he is without a doubt the Antichrist, and I say that without apology." I agree with him one hundred percent. The Bible is clearly telling us throughout its pages that Judas is more than just a sinner that betrayed Jesus. He was the man of sin that wasn't capable of telling the truth. I hope that showing you his true dark side will shine a light and uncover what the Word of God is telling us about this man.

9. The ninth major reason that leads me to believe that Judas was the Devil, or the Antichrist, is the fact that their lives are almost exactly the same. Their patterns are alike, their attitudes parallel each other, their motives are similar, and the way in which they sinned is comparable. Their ability to deceive the multitudes are amazing, they both loved money and being in the spotlight, they both are false preachers, they both have the ability to perform miracles, they have charisma, are both of a mixed descent, and they are filled with pride. They both fulfill scripture about them as lost men, they both are born in hell, they both have a ministry of three and a half years before they are exposed, and the list goes on and on. Also, as we have said, Judas and the Antichrist are the only two men who carry the label of the Son of Perdition. They are the only two men in whom the Devil entered into. They are the only two people that have the title of the Power of Darkness. They are predestinated men, but most of all they are both guilty of betraying Jesus, the Son of God. Judas betrayed Jesus for thirty pieces of silver, while the Antichrist will break his covenant and proclaim to be God. When you look at the life of Judas Iscariot in comparison to the Antichrist you will find that no one else is as comparable or has as much in common as these two men do.

10. The tenth and final reason why I hold to this belief of Judas being the Antichrist is simple. When I sit back and ponder how that out of every human that has ever lived, God saw fit to choose Judas Iscariot to be the Man of Destiny to betray His only begotten Son. It is a no-brainer for me. When I think of the greatest sin ever committed throughout the history of time, in God's eyes, it is the betrayal of Jesus Christ. There is no doubt in my mind that this sin of betraying the innocent Blood of Jesus is the greatest sin in the history of mankind. If you want to get in trouble quick, just start mocking the things of God and the Blood of Jesus. There have been two men when it is all said and done that will be guilty of this great transgression. One of course is Judas and the other, you guessed it, is the Antichrist. When the Antichrist commits this sin in the

Tribulation Period, it will be a slap in the face to what Jesus did on the cross and will ultimately be the straw that breaks the camels back (so to speak). In Daniel 11:24-27, God will bring judgement like this world has never seen because the blood of Jesus is the most important thing there has ever been.

There you have it – ten major reasons why Judas is the Devil's son and part of the unholy trinity that will rear their ugly heads during the Tribulation Period. I hope, after reading these reasons, it has opened your eyes to who Judas really is.

---

[1] Proverbs 9:18
[2] Romans 1:28
[3] Mark 5
[4] Acts 5

THE FORERUNNER

When you begin to look at the life of Jesus and the Devil, you will find that Jesus will always be supreme in that situation. God created the Devil and therefore He is his God – whether the Devil likes it or not. What you will find all through the Word of God and even in our everyday life, is the Devil always trying to steal the glory away from Jesus. For example, Christmas was created to celebrate the birth of Jesus. The Devil has turned around and led people to believe that Christmas is all about gifts, presents, and fun. The Devil teaches that gifts don't come from Jesus, but that they come from Santa Claus. That is a lie straight out of hell. The Bible says in the Book of James 1:17 that every good gift comes from God, not Santa. When we celebrate Easter, it is designed to magnify

Christ for conquering death and rising from the dead. However, as we know, Satan has turned it into the Easter bunny and candy to take the glory away from Jesus.

In the Word of God, often you will find that everything God creates, the Devil copies. The Devil is the master deceiver and he will do everything in his power to go against the Savior. My dad taught a lesson one time on the fact that the Devil is the great counterfeiter. In other words, what God created for good, the Devil will simulate it for evil. The Bible says in the Book of II Corinthians 11:13-15 that Satan is able to transform himself into an angel of light if need be, to trick or deceive you. This pattern has never changed with the Devil and it never will.

With that being said, as Jesus had a forerunner in John the Baptist to proclaim the good news and prepare the way of the lord, you better believe that Satan has a forerunner to prepare his coming; his name is Barack Hussein Obama. Something to notice about the forerunner of Jesus was the fact that John and Jesus were so much alike in the way they preached and conducted themselves, that people could not even tell a difference between the two of them. They even called John the Baptist, "The Messiah." Are you aware of the fact that Obama is so much like the Antichrist that lost people were calling him "The Messiah?" during the elections. There is a Major reason for this. Consider the following: John the Baptist was chosen of God to be His forerunner in the Book of Malachi 3:1. John was filled with the Holy Ghost from his mother's womb. He was ordained before he was born, by God Himself, and was filled with His power. The reason for this is because God wanted everyone to know that when they seen John for the first time, they would see a preacher that they have never seen before. He was to be noted as being totally different than any other preacher they had seen up to that point.

God was trying to get the people to see that John and Jesus had the same exact message and that visually you could see that the forerunner and the Son of God were nearly the same in the way they acted. Even though John's ministry was short, he was on a mission to get people to see who the true Messiah really was, and that they needed to repent. John's humble spirit and over-flowing power was a picture of the Lamb of God that "taketh away the sins of the world" in John 1:29. What I'm simply trying to say is that John the Baptist was chosen by God to point the Jew to their true Messiah (the Lord Jesus Christ). Jesus said that John was the greatest man ever born among women and this was because when people saw John, they saw Jesus. John may not have been popular in his day but he fulfilled his job as the forerunner, and that was his purpose in life.

I want to remind you once again that everything God originates, the Devil imitates. Just like Jesus had a forerunner setting the stage for His ministry, the Devil also has a forerunner ordained right out of hell. As John's life was similar to that of Jesus, Barack Obama's life is similar to that of the Antichrist. The Bible says in the Book of II Thessalonians 2:7 that the mystery of iniquity doth already work. Fifty years ago in America, Barack Hussein Obama would have been laughed out of this country. However, God has turned this country over to Satan because we have forgotten Him[1] and embraced sin. We, as a country, have made this choice and it has opened the door for Satan's forerunner to take charge and set the stage for the Antichrist.

Just as John the Baptist was on a mission to point people to Jesus, Obama is also on a mission to work as fast as he can to point people to his messiah. The things that Obama is doing in America are exactly what the Antichrist will be doing in his reign. For example, Obama is a humanist. He loves the sodomites, he's for gun control, he has charisma, he hates God, he is a big liar, is for a one world government, for a one world currency, is very corrupt, loves money and power, is a reprobate, hates Israel, is a total fake, and the list goes on and on. When people looked at John, they could see Jesus. When you look at Obama, you can see the Antichrist.

The first time I ever laid eyes on Barack Hussein Obama was during the democratic debate between himself and Hillary Clinton. Everything about this man was fresh and new because it was the first time I had ever seen him before. However, the truth is when I started to listen to him and saw the way he acted and spoke (not knowing anything about him), I told everyone in the room that this could be the Antichrist or his forerunner. What I said was very bold and risky, but something struck me about this man and the Holy Ghost would not leave me alone. I have never said that about anyone before and everyone in the room thought I was crazy. I can still remember the night that he became president and how he totally fooled this nation. I was troubled in my spirit and I remember after watching his speech, seeing his proud looks and confident demeanor, I looked at the clock and it was 2:30 a.m. in the morning. I recall my brother coming home and asking me what I was still doing up. I looked at him with a countenance of fear, and told him that America has just elected the forerunner to the Antichrist. I can still remember him laughing at me and thinking I was crazy. May I say that as I am writing this book, my brother and anybody who knows the Bible at all are not laughing now! Obama fits the description of the forerunner perfectly.

Something we should understand about the two forerunners is that their attitude and mindset of who they are serving is exactly the same. John would magnify Jesus and say things like, "I must decrease and He must increase.[2]" Satan's forerunner has the mindset that he must increase, and God must decrease. John was the greatest because he was content with being in the shadows, wanting no credit, while Jesus received all the glory. Mr. Obama, on the other hand, will give Jesus no credit; he, in turn, will give himself all the tribute. When we look at John, he was humble like his Messiah; when you look at Obama, he is proud like *his* messiah.

Another thing to remember about John is the fact that though he was a man, because he was so much like Jesus, he had his own disciples or followers. Obama is the same way, as he also has his own disciples or supporters to help him carry out his evil deeds. I believe that just like John was filled by the Holy Ghost (his Messiah), Obama is being filled or controlled by a demon spirit that is helping him to perform his ultimate goal. Every chance Obama has, he is mocking the Bible or the things of God, elevating himself like the Devil always seems to do. I say to you that no President in history has passed bills and moved as fast as Barack Hussein Obama. Much like the Antichrist, his goal is to deceive as many as he can because he knows that his time is short.

Please allow me to take a few minutes and show you exactly where these two forerunners appear through the pages of the Word of God. I hope to give you facts from the Bible that will lead you to study and search out these truths for yourself. For those of us that have read the Bible all the way through, we are aware of the fact that John the Baptist was prophesied in the Old Testament (before he ever arrived in the four gospels). There are several different passages of scripture in the Old Testament that tell us he would one day appear as God's forerunner. In my mind, the clearest passage is found in the Book of Malachi 3: 1-3. When you come to the New Testament pages, you will quickly find that John the Baptist is found in all four gospels. You find his birth in Luke 1:57. In Mark 1: 1-13, you find his ministry.

God clearly gave the world multiple scriptures throughout His blessed book that proclaimed the arrival of His forerunner. However, you will be surprised to discover that God also gave us many different scriptures concerning the Devil's forerunner. Though Barack Hussein Obama's name is never mentioned in the Bible, there are very clear verses found throughout the New Testament that expose the Devil's forerunner. Although I could show multiple verses on this subject, I only wish to show you LAST DAYS SCRIPTURES to prove this point. My reason for doing this is simply because we are, no doubt, in the end times and these scriptures apply to the church age. The Bible teaches us in I Timothy 4: 1-2 that ONLY in the last days will there be an out-pouring of demonic spirits like never before. Timothy tells us in verse 2 that in the latter days some will indeed depart from the faith, beginning to give heed to seducing spirits and doctrines of devils. Notice these devil spirits are not unleashed until the last days according to the Bible. Timothy goes on to say in verse 2 that these devils will speak lies in hypocrisy; they will have their conscience seared with a hot iron. In other words, they are not interested in being born again, because they are spiritual zombies and are devilish in their motives. Does that sound like president Obama or what?

The Bible is teaching us that in the end times fallen spirits will come on the scene that have only one purpose in life – to deceive the people and cause them to blaspheme God. Timothy is warning Christians to avoid these kinds of people and to be mindful of their deception.

If you read farther along in your Bible you will find that the apostle Peter, as well as Jude, uncover these ungodly spirits and warn the Christians of their divine purpose. II Peter chapter 2 and also the Book of Jude say nearly the same thing in its message. They are warning the church that there are false teachers in the last days which are evil from the inside out. They describe these types of people as not just the average sinner you will meet on an every day basis, but rather fallen spirits that are beyond help and hope. Peter, as well as Jude, describe how these people are wells without water and are reserved in the blackness of darkness, forever. What they are telling us through these verses is that there are demon possessed spirits that have been loosed out of hell during these last days to cause pain and hurt to all that they come in contact with. The Bible says in Jude, verse 4 that there are certain men that have crept in unawares, who were **before of old, ordained to condemnation**.

Also in II Peter 2:3, it talks about how they with feigned words, shall make merchandise of you: **whose judgement lingereth not, and their damnation slumbereth not.**

The Bible is simply expressing to us that there are certain people, through the help of Satan that **have secretly** come to the forefront to torment mankind. It's amazing when you sit down and study these two powerful chapters, both writers connect the angels that sinned with these false teachers. When I think about men that "crept in unawares who were before of old ordained to this condemnation," Mr. Obama comes to my mind without hesitation. It seems like nobody knows where he is from because all that information is hidden. It's a sad day in the United States of America when a man can run for President without the proof of a birth certificate. However, what's even sadder than this is the fact that there is still no birth certificate after a year of being President. Satan has this country blinded to who this man really is. Consider the following: if you were caught speeding and an officer pulled you over to ask for your license, you would have no problem showing it to him if you had it in your possession. The problem with Mr. Obama is that he is not from this country and if he were, then he would have nothing to hide. Even his own wife in a public speech accidentally confessed that his hometown was in Kenya. If that were true, then it would disqualify him from being the President of this country.

My dad sent me an article that exposed Mr. Obama even a step further. According to Mr. Obama, he said that he attended a certain college for 4 years and made a lot of friends in the process. This article said that they interviewed a number of different students and teachers from the college where Mr. Obama supposedly attended and not one of them ever recall seeing or talking to him. The article also said there was no yearbook picture or any remembrance of him at all. Who is Barack Hussein Obama? Could he be a forerunner of Satan to set the stage for the Antichrist?

If you read other verses throughout II Peter and Jude you will find that these evil men will speak with great swelling words of vanity to deceive the people. These men will talk a big game but they are lying to you the whole time. They can make you believe every word through charisma, but all the time they are deceiving you. In other words, they will tell you anything you want to hear as long as you will follow their ungodly agenda. Mr. Obama is a perfect example of what I am talking about. I beg you to read these two chapters in great detail the next time you study your Bible. I promise you that the more you read these chapters, the more you will see the forerunner of Satan. In my opinion, there is no better description of a man that fits these verses than Barack Hussein Obama. He and his followers are very dark and their intentions are not good. Please do your homework on this messenger of Satan, and you will soon find out that what I'm speaking is truth from God's written Word, and not my opinion. So as we have clearly seen, not only is John the Baptist found throughout the Bible but Mr. Obama is found as well.

Another thing that amazes me about John is the fact that he was chosen of God to be the forerunner of Jesus. He appears six months before Jesus – in other words, directly in front of Jesus. John showed up right on time, like the Bible teaches. It was ordained of God that shortly after John came, here comes the Lord. Also, when

John was preparing His way, the world was in total ruin. They were killing babies and were blinded to their sin. The world was wicked and evil, and the government was in horrible shape. I'm telling you that when John started his ministry, the world was in a total search for someone that had all the answers. Then Jesus came, the one who John has been announcing the entire time. Just like I said before, it is a sign of things to come. Similar to the forerunner of God, the timing will be exactly the same for Satan's predecessor. Think about the horrible shape our world is in. We are still killing babies, we are blinded to our sin, we are wicked, and the government is in terrible order. The Devil's forerunner is moving fast because it will not be long before it's time for the Antichrist to appear with seemingly "all the world's answers." Christians, this is how I know that Jesus is coming back again to take us out of here in the near future. Also, when Jesus comes the third time to set up his thousand year millennial reign, it will be the exact same pattern. He will have to straighten out everything again.

There is one more thing to remember about the two forerunners that is very important. What we have to remember about John, the first forerunner, is that when everything was accomplished and Jesus began his ministry, John's ministry had to end. The reason for this is because his job was complete and he needed to be removed so that the people would only see their Messiah, Jesus Christ. Shortly after Jesus arrives, John is beheaded. The same thing must happen with the Devil's forerunner. When Obama's job is finally complete and he has done what Satan needs, then he will have to be removed so that the Antichrist can be the only ruler of the world. I want you to mark it down, and remember this. When the forerunner's job is over and the Antichrist is revealed, then Obama will quickly disappear and the Antichrist will rule the world. The fact is, John the Baptist was only the forerunner (and not part of the trinity), so he had to be removed so Jesus would receive all the glory. Mr. Obama will also have to get out of the way as the forerunner, so that the unholy trinity will get all the glory[3].

There is one last bit of information about the two forerunners that we should see. John and Jesus are both Jewish, while President Obama and Judas are both mixtures of different races. We will talk about this more in chapter number 9.

I sure hope I was a help to you in the facts about Satan's forerunner. Barack Hussein Obama was the worst decision America has ever made, but there is a great possibility that he is fulfilling scripture – just like John the Baptist did in the ministry of Jesus Christ.

---

[1] Psalms 9:17
[2] John 3:30
[3] Daniel 11:20-21

WHAT WILL THE ANTICHRIST LOOK LIKE? HOW WILL HE ACT?

When it comes to the topic of what the Antichrist will look like in the time he is revealed, there are so many different views or opinions, by many different people. The main reason for this is because there are very few times that the Antichrist is described in the Word of God. The Bible is not very clear on exactly what the Antichrist physically will look like, only on what his demeanor or personality will be. That leads people to speculate or give their opinion of how he will appear. Of course, when man puts his spin on it, the chance that it will match up with the Bible is almost impossible. The only thing I know to do when it comes to giving you a picture of what the Antichrist will look like is to give you Bible verses that deal with the subject.

Many people tend to think the Antichrist will have a bad right eye. The reason many believe this theory is because in Zechariah 11:17, the Bible says that his right eye shall be utterly darkened, referring to the Antichrist. I know of so many Christians that tend to believe this description is referring to his actual physical eye. I could not disagree more, and I think they are totally wrong. The Bible is clear that this verse is simply referring to his nature, or attitude relating to his evil spirit. In Proverbs 28:22 it says, "He that hasteneth to be rich hath an evil eye." Does that sound like Judas or what? The whole time Judas followed Jesus his mind was controlled by the love of money. In I Timothy 6:10 the Bible says the love of money is the root of all evil. This verse tells us that if your mind is consumed with riches, then your spirit will be dark and your eye will look toward evil. Also, in Matthew 6:22-23 Jesus says that "The light of the body is in the eye, if therefore thine eye be single, thy whole body shall have light." In other words, if your eye is focused on Jesus all the days of your life, then your whole body will follow. However, on the flip side, verse twenty-three states that "if thine eye be evil, thy whole body shall be full of darkness, therefore if the light that be in thee be darkness, how great is that darkness." The Bible is speaking about his mindset or his nature,

If you study the Bible, there will be nothing at all wrong with his appearance. In Isaiah 14:10-13 the Bible speaks of Lucifer falling from heaven and going from the most fair to look upon to the lowest that a created being could possibly go. God made Lucifer as the most beautiful creation He had ever created but because of disobedience, he fell from God's grace and went to hell. With Judas being who he is, there's no doubt in my mind that the Antichrist will be fair to look upon, or easy on the eyes. Just like in heaven before his fall and just like in the days of Judas when he walked with Jesus, the Antichrist will be over flowing with charisma, the ability to deceive, and the talent to smooth-talk the world. Judas had no problem deceiving God's chosen few or anyone else he came in contact with while he was on earth. He fooled men that Jesus, Himself was teaching on a daily basis. What makes you think he will not be able to fool this godless world without the presence of the Holy Ghost anywhere to be found during the Tribulation Period?

Judas has already taken notes from the greatest teacher known to man in his earthly ministry. He walked with Jesus Christ for three and a half years while following the footprints of the Savior. He learned everything about his life, his gestures, his mannerisms, the way he healed people, the way he performed miracles, and so on and so forth. Judas will imitate and try to be exactly like Jesus in every way possible. I want you to remember that this is the time of Jacob's trouble[1] and that the Tribulation Period is meant for the Jews. This is because they cried out, "Let his blood be upon us and our children," in Matthew 27:25. God will fulfill that Scripture in Revelations, chapters 6-20 as the blood of untold millions will flow throughout that period of time for their rejection of Christ. The Jews are still looking for their messiah, and they will look at the Antichrist, and will say to themselves, "This must be the messiah because of the way he looks and the way that he conducts himself."

Another reason they will accept him as their messiah is because of the miracles, signs, and wonders that he will have the power to perform. Jesus always had a problem with the Jews in His day because most of them could care less about preaching and very few (if any of them), really loved Him. The Jews always desired to see some kind of miracle or sign from Him. Jesus would always rebuke them and say to them that "…a wicked and evil generation seeketh after a sign." Just like Judas had the power to perform miracles in Jesus day, he will captivate the minds of people in the Tribulation Period as well. The Antichrist will seemingly have all the answers that everyone is seeking for. He will look like a Bible character and try to make people believe that he is the messiah. Most people believe that Jesus looked weak, frail, and sort of like a hippie from the 60s while he walked on planet earth. Let me say that this is a total lie. If anyone was a man in its purest sense, Jesus was a man of all men. Jesus had to be a strong man because nobody else could have physically gone through what he did without being a 'man's man.' The Lord went through five mock trails and the crucifixion.

Any other human would have never made it as long as He did. There is no debating the fact that Jesus was a strong, powerful man.

On the other hand, the Antichrist is very smart and he knows what the Jews are seeking. Remember that they are blinded to the fact that Jesus already came. They rejected their Messiah and have a totally different idea of what he will be and look like. The Bible says in Isaiah 53:2 concerning Jesus that there was nothing that should be desired of Him. To simply state, when the Jews looked at Jesus, they did not see their Messiah. There was nothing special about Jesus physically because He humbled Himself and took on the form of a man[2]. However, the Bible says in II Corinthians 11:13-15 that Satan, himself can transform into an angel of light. When the Antichrist comes on the scene, in reality he will look exactly opposite of Jesus. Because the Jews are blinded, they will see his glory, power, and majesty, and they will proclaim to one another that this must be God.

The Jews have always glorified in appearance, but God looketh upon the heart. When the Jewish people viewed their King, they did not see Him in a manger; they only saw Him on a throne. They did not like the way Jesus came, but they will love the way the Antichrist will come. The fact is because they rejected Jesus, they are blinded to the Antichrist and his evil plan. The Jewish race will suffer heartache and bloodshed like they never have before. The Antichrist will deceive the hearts of the people and will appear to resemble Jesus but, in reality, he will be the total opposite. The Antichrist will be beautiful, radiant, charismatic, glorious, and powerful. As a result, all the people will bow at his feet.

Another aspect that the Antichrist will possess is a genius mind. The Antichrist will be the smartest man that has ever lived beside Jesus Christ, Himself. What I don't think most people realize is that the Antichrist, the false prophet, and the Devil are all part of the same trinity. They are all working together to deceive and destroy as many people as they can, as fast as they can. Because the Antichrist and the Devil are the same, they have devised a master plan that is six thousand years in the making and will be executed, to perfection, during the Tribulation Period. Since the beginning of time Satan has been walking to and fro, up and down the earth, seeking whom he may devour[3]. When we are fast asleep, the Devil is wide awake, staying one step ahead of the game.

The Devil was created as a very special angel in the sight of God. He was in charge of the music in heaven and God blessed Lucifer with many different qualities in Glory. However, pride got the best of Satan and he fell from his lofty position to the pits of hell. From that time until the present, Satan is always thinking of ways to destroy people's lives and has been laying out traps and snares for fallen man for six thousand years. I Timothy 3:6-7 tells us that you need to walk very carefully with God every day because, if you're not careful, you will be lifted up with pride and will fall into condemnation, into the snare of the Devil. Simply put, you will fall into a trap that the Devil has set up for you. That's why the Bible warns us in Ephesians 5:15 that we need to walk circumspectly *(or exactly)*, not as fools, but as wise.

The Devil is an expert at ruining people's lives and getting them to fall as a reproach and a disaster in the sight of God. The Bible says in Ephesians 2:2 that Satan is the prince and power of the air, and is in control of this earth, for the time being. The Devil has studied human life for thousands of years and knows exactly the mindset of man. People really think they can play around with sin and challenge the Devil head-on. I say to those people that they are fools and don't know the Bible. The only way Christians can handle the Devil is to do what Jesus did in the Book of Matthew chapter 4. When he was dealing with the Devil, Jesus gave us the answer by praying, fasting, and using the Word of God. That is the only way anybody has a chance against the Devil. Outside of being filled with the Spirit of God, we are no match for the Devil. Most people are so weak spiritually, that they are taken captive by Satan at his own will, like the Bible teaches.

Satan is described as the author of confusion meaning – he invented it (found in I Corinthians 14:33). Also, he is the father of lies in John 8:44, the accuser of the brethren in Job chapter 1, a roaring lion, and The Power of Darkness. He is known as the Prince of the Air and the Master Deceiver. With all that being said, it is safe to say that he is a force to be reckoned with and without the presence of the Holy Ghost, the people of the Tribulation Period have no chance to out-wit or out-do the Antichrist.

This has been the plan of Satan since time began – a world without the Spirit of God, and his own power and time to reign. It will be short lived, but the Devil will have his time to shine and to carry out his master plan. As we know, the Antichrist will have all the answers for the first three and a half years, much like Judas did. However, after that time is up, his true colors will begin to show and the world will see the Devil take control overnight. He will turn from not offending people to offending everyone and anyone who does not worship him as god. In Daniel 11:36-37, you will finally see his true beliefs unfold before your very eyes. He will reveal himself and the world will realize that they have been deceived, but by this time it is too late. He has already taken the world as his own and if you dare to rise up against him you will be murdered on the spot, as an example for the rest of the world. For the first three and a half years, he has had every answer known to man; in the last three and a half years, he will blaspheme the God of heaven and will worship the god of force, or nature. He will sit down on the throne of David and claim to be God while all the time he is the Devil. He will be wholly against God, and God will finally have had enough. He will judge and slay him with the Sword of his mouth in the battle of Armageddon. At that time, Jesus will rule with a rod of iron and to His kingdom there shall be no end[4].

With all that being said, the Antichrist will be absolutely brilliant and "blow the minds" of the people for the first three and a half years, because he has seemingly all the answers. He will also be of a mixed descent and will appeal to all races and beliefs. He will look very unique and different. He will stick out among the crowd. If you will study the Bible or even history books, you will find that Judas is from a place called Kerioth. The land of Kerioth is a city in Moab, located next to Ammon and Edom; it is just above Egypt. If you study the Book of Genesis, you will find that the Ammonites and the Moabites are a cursed seed, created through the sin of Lots two daughters. These women got their father drunk so that they could bare seed through him. The Moabites and Ammonites have and always will carry the curse of God with them through the sin of Lot's two daughters.

These two races are descendants of the Ishmaelite or Arabic, as we know them today. The Ishmaelite was also formed through the sin of Abraham, who got impatient with God and slept with his wife's Egyptian handmaiden, Hagar − rather than with his own wife, Sarai. This was never in the plan of God and as a result God cursed this seed, and the Ishmael or Arab seed was born. Ishmael is a mixture of Jewish and Egyptian blood, and is a corrupt seed. The Moabites and Ammonites are descendants of the Ishmaelites and mixtures of different races, as well. As a result of Abraham's sin, God put a curse on Ishmael's race until the end of time. The Bible tells us that Ishmael will be a wild man and never able to co-exist with other races. He will live off other people's land until the end of time[5]. If you know anything about the Bible (and history for that matter), you understand that the Ishmaelites are living on 90% of the Promised Land that was given to the Jew through the seed of Isaac.

The Moabites, Ammonites, Edomites, and other various countries are a good example of what God said about the Ishmaelites. The Arabs think it is their land because of Ishmael but God says it is Israel's land through the promised seed, Isaac. The Arab people are a mixture of other races and are cursed by God. It's amazing how *Judas'* birth came through a cursed seed. The Moabites are half Jew and half Moab as a result of sin. Thank God, we understand that Jesus came through the womb of Mary and was of the promised seed of Isaac[6].

God is showing us, through the birth of Judas and his Moabite roots, that he was cursed even from his foundation. Through the birth of Christ, God is showing us that He is blessed even from His foundation as a promised seed, through God's chosen people (the Jew). The Jews and Arabs have been fighting over one question since the beginning of time. This question is simply, "Who is God's chosen people? The Jews or the Arabs?" The Arabs believe it's their land because Ishmael was born fourteen years before Isaac. However, Israel believes it is *their* land because God promised it to them through the birth of Isaac. This question will be answered during the Tribulation Period. We understand that the Antichrist is also of a mixed descent, much like Judas is. The Antichrist is part Jew and part Arab as well and will work with both parties during the Tribulation Period. As we know, he will set up a covenant between the two, only to break it three and a half years later through a false peace. Once he turns his back on the Jews, the Book of Zechariah teaches that he will break his ties with them and rage war against them. The Antichrist will gather all his descendants against Israel and, because he is of that cursed seed, he will have the one-world army behind him.

In the heart of every Ishmaelite burns a deep hatred for the Jews because they are the blessed seed. The Antichrist will then fulfill every Arabs dream of destroying the Jew once and for all. He tries to kill every living Jew through the Battle of Armageddon. When the Antichrist and his followers finally think they will destroy them, God will show up right on time and show the entire world that Israel has always been God's people, just like the Bible says. I think it is pretty amazing how Judas and the Antichrist are both from the same part of the world, and are formed through sin and rebellion. They are both Ishmaelites and are cursed by God.

There is one more thing about the Moabite race that is worth noting. When you look at who they are, the Moabites are known (by historians) as a peaceful group of people on the outside, but a very wicked group of people on the inside. When you study what the Moabite people believe spiritually, it will make you sick to your stomach. The Moabites are well known for serving a god by the name of "Chemosh." This style of worship is nothing more than another form of devil worship. The Moabite people would get together and pray to their god, Chemosh under demonic influences. Once they were filled with the spirit of Satan, they would offer up the sacrifice of children to be burned alive in order to please their god. In other words, what they believed in their heart was different from what you could see with your eyes.

The Moabites seemed peaceful when you looked at them, but their hearts raged war that only Satan could satisfy. When I think about the mindset that the Moabites had it reminds me that this is the same mindset Judas and the Antichrist hold onto. When you look at these two with the natural eye, they seem peaceful and harmless; but if you could see what is going on in their heart, you would discover that Satan is in complete control of their life. When I start to think about how Judas grew up as a Moabite, there is no telling how many times as a young man, that he was a part of this satanic worship with his fellow countrymen. This proves that Judas was around the presence of Satan, even when he was a little boy. From the start of Judas' life until the end, we can see a constant influence of the Devil from his Moabite roots. Judas was familiar with demonic activity as a young boy, a teenager, and as a follower of Jesus. Judas was a Devil from the beginning.

The Moabite race wanted to be one thing in public and another thing in private. The Bible has always condemned this belief and teaches that Jesus is the only true God[7]. May I say that this is the very definition of Judas Iscariot. Please be careful not to follow a man from what you see on the outside, but always remember to look at their motives first. The Antichrist will also have this same mindset and will seem like he wants peace with the Jews. All the while he wants evil to rule this earth and the God of Israel to be over-thrown. So we clearly see that Judas, through his cursed foundation as a Moabite, will be over flowing with Demonic charisma and will deceive the Jews that he hates through lying wonders.

Another thing that God is showing us through his mixed descent is that, not only will he appeal to the Jews, but to the whole world as well. There will be no such thing as doctrine; everybody will "love" one another. The whole world will operate under a one-world system that he has set up and will reach out to all races and all religions. The Bible says in I Thessalonians 5:2 that "…When they say peace, peace, then sudden destruction cometh." The Jews hated Jesus and rejected his spirit filled preaching, refusing to accept Him as their Messiah. In turn, God will give them what they wanted – a false christ that will take many of them to hell through miracles and deception.

There is one more important factor that I want to bring to your attention when we talk about the Antichrist being of a mixed descent. If you will read the Book of Isaiah, Chapter 10, verses 5 through 34 (along with the rest of Isaiah), you will find many references that explain how the Antichrist will come from the Assyrian Empire. When you study the history and origins of Assyria, you will find that their existence first began through inter-mixed marriages with other races. Much like Judas Iscariot is a mixture of Moab and Jewish blood, the Antichrist will be of the same mixture. If you were to study a Bible map and the Assyrian Empire, you would see that its territory runs from southwest Asia all the way down to the land of Egypt. Contained within its borders you will find the Ammonites, the Edomities and (of course) the Moabites, where Judas was born two thousand years ago. Out of all the places that the Antichrist could come from, isn't it amazing that the Bible says that he will come from the same exact territory that Judas did?

It's stunning just how large earth is when you really stop to think about it. If you were to view a globe of the earth and look at the depth, the height, and the length it would probably shock you to the maximum degree. For example, if you were to drive from Belleville, Michigan to Daytona Beach, Florida it would take you twenty hours (non-stop at seventy M.P.H.), before you reached your destination. After finally arriving in Florida, you would discover that you only traveled about two to three inches on the face of a globe. This planet is massive and to think that the Antichrist and Judas were born in the exact same area should really tell us something. Just like Judas was born of a corrupt seed, so is the Antichrist.

Another thing to discover about the Assyrian Empire is the fact that they are known for their strong-willed natures and their amazing fighting ability. The Assyrians even to this day are well known as the most brutal and vicious warriors this world has ever seen. They rely on their own abilities and are very independent in their spirits. The Bible teaches that they will kill just to kill, and they refuse to obey the authorities that are set over them. They are known as pagans in their worship and, like I have already said, they are of a mixed descent and a dark complexion. War will always be in their hearts and peace they will never find. They are very selfish and very prideful. In closing out this thought concerning the appearance of the Antichrist, I have come to the conclusion that the greatest example of what the Antichrist will be and look like is what we have already covered in chapter eight of this book. Remember, in chapter eight, when I said that the forerunner would simulate the Antichrist in every way, possibly much like John did with Jesus? The next time you watch Barack Hussein Obama give a speech or pass a law, remember the qualities of the Antichrist as you watch him.

The Bible teaches in Psalms 9:17 and various other scriptures that "…Every nation that forgets God will be turned into hell," and America will be no exception to the rule. Who would have ever dreamed in the United States of America that we, as a people, would elect an inter-racial Muslim President that hates God and the Bible. The election of Barrack Hussein Obama is nothing short of the judgment of God on this country. The Bible teaches all throughout its pages that sin has a payment involved with it. Sin must be paid for according to Romans 6:23 and God is showing us – through the election of Barack Hussein Obama – that pay-day has finally come for America.

When I think about the judgement of God in the Bible, my mind thinks about America and all her sin. We understand that God destroyed two whole cities in the Book of Genesis alone over the sin of sodomy. The Bible calls this sin an abomination and it literally makes God sick. He has judged every nation that accepts this life-style, and it has finally caught up with America. There are millions of people that are wrapped up in this vile sin across the country and God has now said enough is enough. I also think about the awful sin of abortion. The Bible teaches that life begins at conception, according to Psalms 51:5. God is the giver of life and He alone is the only one with the right to take it[8]. Abortion is murder, whether we believe it or not. What Adolph Hitler did in Germany during World War II is Sunday school compared to what we are doing in America on a daily basis. Over 60 million babies have been murdered since abortion was created, and it has angered a Sovereign God to the brink of his wrath. America is in the worst shape that it has ever been in, and I believe the Lord is judging this country like never before. It is being judged for its continually unchanging sin and rebellion towards HIS HOLY NAME.

As a result of our transgressions, God has seen fit to send us the worst leader that America has ever known. God has always condemned mixed marriages and inter-racial fellowships. God has always intended whites to marry whites, blacks to marry blacks, Japanese to marry Japanese, and so on and so forth. Often times God has judged people for going outside of their countries and marrying other nationalities in the Scriptures. When Noah stepped off the Ark after the flood (in the Book of Genesis), God made sure that Noah's sons all went to different parts of the world to replenish the earth. All of Noah's sons were sent in different directions and separated by bodies of water. The reason for this is because God wanted their races to be separate and marry after their own kind. God never intended blacks to marry whites and whites to marry blacks (and so on and so forth). I heard a preacher say one time concerning this subject that "you have never seen a robin kiss a bluejay." Just think about that for a minute. Even animals understand this simple truth from the Word of God. Many of you may think I am racist because of this belief, but may I say that these are the words of God, Himself and not me.

Another example of this would have to be Samson in the Old Testament (see Judges, Chapters 13–16). Samson was blessed with great strength and power with God as long as he was following His path. The Bible records that his power was limitless and his future was bright and glorious – as long as he followed his Nazarite Covenant of an unshaven head and marrying within his own people. If you read the story of Samson, you will find that everything was going well until he started following after strange women.

When Samson obeyed his flesh rather than God, his life went downhill in a hurry. God has always cursed inter-racial marriages and judged every nation that accepts it. To think that God has sent us a man that is of a mix descent (who is so much like the Antichrist) to run America, proves that America is under the judgement of God. In closing out this point about the judgement of God being on America for her sin, I want to give you two reasons why I believe God has sent us a president that compares so greatly to the Antichrist.

Up to this point in the book, nearly everything that I have said has been fact from the Word of God, without my opinion. However, these two points will be my opinion. There are two reasons why I firmly believe God has sent us Barack Hussein Obama in these last days. Number one is a point that we have already discussed in chapter eight. I believe that Obama is the forerunner to the Antichrist and he must fulfil his purpose as a forerunner, setting the stage for his appearance. The second reason I believe God has seen fit to raise up Mr. Obama in America is to give us a glimpse of what is about to follow in the Tribulation Period. Could it be that God is sending a warning before the Tribulation Period? Many times in the Bible God will send a warning before His mighty hand sends divine judgement.

When I look at Barack Hussein Obama and how he carries himself, my mind almost always thinks of the Antichrist. God has sent us a leader that emulates the Antichrist to perfection. I believe God is sending many warning signs all across the world that time is just about over and we need to heed the warning. God is trying to show us, through Barack Hussein Obama's leadership, that his agenda will lead us right into the Antichrist's hands, if we don't repent and get right with God. Think about it – God used Jeremiah for fifty-two chapters to warn the people of Israel that judgment would come if they didn't repent; nobody would listen to Jeremiah. God used Noah for one hundred and twenty years to warn the world about the flood; only his family got on the Ark. God sent two angels to rescue Lot and his family before judgment hit Sodom and Gomorrah; everybody else died.

In the case of America, I believe that God has sent us a picture of what the Antichrist will be like and, if we don't heed the warning, shame on us. Let me plainly say, sinner friend, that God is sending one final warning and He is using Barack Hussein Obama to do it. Please get right with God before it's too late[9].

I hope that we have seen a picture of what the Antichrist will be like throughout this chapter. He will be brilliant, he will be beautiful, he will be charismatic, he will be mixed, he will look very unique, he will perform miracles, he will appeal to all people, and he will seemingly have all the answers. However, in the end (much like Judas), he will be a master deceiver, he will be a murderer, and he will be lost.

---

[1] Jeremiah 30:7
[2] Philippians 2:7-8
[3] Job 1:7
[4] Luke 1:32
[5] Genesis 16:11-12
[6] Genesis 17:19 and John 1:11
[7] Matthew 6:24
[8] Zechariah 1:5
[9] Isaiah 1:18

THE CONCEPT THAT JUDAS COULD NOT BE THE ANTICHRIST

There are so many people in the Christian circle that have been trained and taught against the fact that Judas could be the Antichrist. Most people have no Bible verses to refute it. However, that will not stop them from arguing with you anyway. I believe a lot of people are so steeped in religion, tradition, or the way that they have been taught that it doesn't matter how many Bible verses you show them, for they know what they have been taught and it is hard to change their minds. When you try to tell people about Jesus and witness for the cause of Christ, you can show them from the Bible that Jesus is the only way to heaven. You can prove that unless they accept Him as their Savior, they will go to hell. Most people, however, will disregard the Scriptures and will say things like, "I don't care what the Bible says; I know what I have been taught." Let me clearly say that when someone has that attitude, they are blinded to the truth because the Bible is right and they are wrong – whether they believe it or not.

It is the same concept with Judas. Many people tend to think that Judas could not be the Antichrist because they hold to the fact that God would never bring someone back from the dead during the Tribulation Period. I say to those people that God can do whatever He wants to do. As a matter of fact, He already has, during the earthly ministry of Jesus. In Matthew 17:1-5, the Bible tells us how Jesus was totally transformed on top of the mount. The Lord was so pleased with the service of Peter, James, and John that He wanted to reveal to them what no one had seen before. Jesus took them up high on the mountain, away from the rest of the crowd, and was transfigured before their very eyes as He showed them His Glory. The Bible is clear that Moses and Elijah appeared to minister unto them as well.

Moses had already been dead for hundreds of years but God brought him back to minister unto these three men of God. That alone is proof that God can do whatever He wants when it comes to revealing Himself unto man. What's so amazing about this is that during the Tribulation Period, in the Book of Revelation 11:3-17, Moses and Elijah appear as God's two witnesses or candlesticks, at that time. They are literally God's only two preachers to stand against the evil of that day. I personally believe what God is doing by using these two prophets again to be a light in a dark world, is to simply fulfill Bible Scripture once again.

In the gospel of Luke 16: 27-31 we read an account of Lazarus and the rich man. This is the famous chapter in the Bible where the rich man dies and goes to hell. In verse 27, the rich man said unto Father Abraham, "I pray therefore that thou wouldest send him to my father's house, for I have five brethren, that he may testify unto them, lest they also come into this place of torment." Basically, he was asking for a miracle, some kind of angel, or even Lazarus to appear unto his family to warn them about hell. However, the

Bible records that Abraham answered, "They have Moses and the prophets; let them hear them." What Abraham was saying to him is that they already have the writings of Moses and the prophets, and if they will not listen to their preaching then they would not believe, even if one of them rose from the dead. The rich man, much like a lot of other people, wanted a miracle or a sign but he refused to believe the Bible.

When we get to the Tribulation Period, God will fulfill that scripture because Moses and Elijah, themselves will be preaching to the Jewish people in person, trying to win them to Jesus. Moses and Elijah are, without a doubt, the two most popular and well renowned prophets in the whole Old Testament. When you talk to a Jew about Jesus in the New Testament, it will be just like talking to a wall after only a couple of seconds. To the Jew, the New Testament is hogwash and unimportant, because they are blinded to the fact that Jesus already came. If you want to break through to a Jew, you must use Old Testament scriptures for it is the standard by which they live.

Moses wrote the first five books of the Old Testament, while Elijah did miracles and had power like no other man, outside of Jesus.

God will fill them with unlimited power while they are preaching and the Jews will view this on a daily basis. As a result, the Jews will hate them and wish they were dead. These two men will die and their bodies will be laid in the streets for the entire world to see. The Bible says that the Jews, along with the rest of the world, will rejoice and have parties because they are finally dead and out of their lives for good. This will prove Luke 16: 27-32 and fulfill the scriptures that say, "...That though one rose from the dead, yet they would not believe."

Just as those verses will be a fulfilling of the scripture with Moses and Elijah, I believe that Judas (being the Antichrist), will also fulfill the Scriptures. There are a couple reasons I hold to this belief. First of all, I believe this because Jesus called Judas the Son of Perdition in the garden, and the Bible calls the Antichrist the Son of Perdition as well. This will fulfill the Scriptures and prove that this is the same person when Judas comes on the scene. I believe this because Jesus is "...the Way, the Truth, and the Life." He gave Judas this title that will never change, and therefore he must fulfill his it in the days to come.

Secondly, I believe that Judas has to be the Antichrist in order to fulfill scripture because of the statement Jesus made about him in Mark 14:21. He made probably the most unusual statement ever recorded in the entire Word of God. Jesus said, "...The Son of Man goeth as it is written of him: but, Woe to that man in whom the Son of Man is betrayed." He could have stopped right there. Following this however, he says, "It is good for that man if he had never been born." What a strange statement made by the Son of God, or was it? This verse has always spoken to me of future judgement that will take place concerning Judas.

Jesus and Judas will meet again, once and for all finishing the war between Jesus and the Antichrist. After the final judgement, when the Antichrist is exposed that he deceived the nations, he will once and for all be cast into the Lake of Fire. He will be with the Devil and the false prophet, tormented day and night forever. This is where they will be forgotten by God for all of eternity. They will then burn forever in the wrath of Almighty God, while the born-again saints enjoy what he once had. Praise the Lord. It is no wonder that Jesus said it was good that he had never been born.

In summary, the concept that Judas could not be the Antichrist is just not true. There are so many truths about Judas throughout the Bible which prove that the Antichrist and he are one and the same. I beg you to not always believe what you hear, but to study the scriptures if you want to find the answers.

We will deal more with this concept later in the book, as I give you a number of different examples where God brings people back from the dead to fulfill His will. The fact of the matter is that God can do whatever He wants to – for He is God. If the Bible says it, then we must believe it.[1]

---

[1] Psalms 12:6-7 and Psalms 119:160

WHY I BELIEVE JUDAS NEVER REPENTED THE BIBLE WAY

When I examine the scriptures concerning Judas Iscariot, there is no way I could ever believe that he repented according to the Bible way. We that understand the Bible know that there are two types of repentance as recorded within its pages.

First of all, there is a Godly repentance found in II Corinthians 7:8-10. This type of repentance is the only kind that God is interested in. We find throughout the Bible that repentance comes from God alone. The two ways that God has chosen to speak with man is through the conviction of the Holy Ghost (for the lost), and to restore fellowship again with a saved man after he has sinned. We find that God, through the spirit, will choose to deal with the heart of man about his soul. He will give him an open door to repent and come to Him on *His* time-table. If a man or woman refuses to accept His invitation, He will stop working with them and deal with someone else. God is looking for man to turn from his sin against his own will, and truly repent the Biblical way. When God brings a man to the point of salvation, that man has a decision to make. Do I repent God's way, or do I wait for a more convenient season like King Agrippa did, in Acts chapter 26? When a man is truly in a state of contrition and he exercises repentance according to the Bible, you will see a definite change and a desire to walk with Jesus. God has only chosen one way to deal with the heart of man and that is through true Godly sorrow that worketh repentance.

A good example of a man that repented God's way is found in Luke 18:10-14. In those verses you will find a man that God had smote with conviction and true repentance. It is there that the publican was so remorseful over his lost condition that he would not so much as lift his eyes unto heaven; but he smote upon his breast and said, "God be merciful unto me, a sinner." Jesus was so pleased with this man's prayer he responded by saying, "This man went down to his house justified." God dealt with this man through Godly repentance, and because he responded when God dealt with him, he lives in heaven today. When you repent the Bible way, you will care less who is around or what you can get out of it. The only thing that matters is that you get right with God. That is how God deals with the lost.

Once a man is saved, the Lord will also deal with him when he has sinned and broken fellowship with God, as found in I John 1:9. God will put a man under conviction until he is willing to repent and get things right with Him. Notice that He is in control and, until a man humbles his heart and repents over his sin, God cannot help him.

We find this type of repentance after a Godly sort in the life of Peter. When Peter denied Christ three times during his earthly trial, he had made a major mistake. However, when Jesus made eye contact with Peter in the judgement hall, found in Luke 22:60-62, the Bible says that Peter went out and wept bitterly because of what he had just done. Peter was truly sorry that he had denied Christ and God knew his heart. We find Peter repenting God's way and not because he had to, but rather because he wanted to. From that time forward, Peter walked closer to God than he had ever walked before. Peter loved Jesus and strived to walk with God until the day he died. There are many other examples found in the Bible regarding Godly repentance and in all those cases you will find transformed lives.

On the other hand, the second kind of repentance that is found in the Bible is after the will of man, and not after the will of God. The Word of God if filled with people that resisted His call and wanted to repent later in life (or on their own schedule). God is not interested in this type of repentance, and He will not hear the prayer of the wicked. A man or woman must humble themselves to be saved when God is dealing and working on them, or they will never get saved.

I think of Esau when I consider man-made repentance and I see someone that was unable to find forgiveness. In the Book of Genesis we find that Esau made a big mistake by selling his birthright to his brother, Jacob for a bowl of lentils. Esau refused the voice of God and failed to repent over what he had done. Later in life, after he had realized the magnitude of his sin, you find in Hebrews 12:16-17 that Esau sought repentance that could only come from God, and couldn't find it. The Bible even said he sought it carefully with tears, but could not. This proves that God is not interested in a man-made repentance, but only in a God-made repentance. This world is filled with people that refuse the call of God because it is uncomfortable at the time; later in life, they try to reach out to God when they are good and ready, but God does not hear anything they have to say.

We see in the life of Judas that he did not repent until he was already condemned, or caught. The Bible is clear in Matthew 27:3 that Judas repented himself, but not after a Godly sort. Nowhere in the life of Judas was he ever truthful or honest up to this point, and this moment was no different. Quickly, I'm going to give you a few reasons why Judas repented in his own timing and not after a Godly fashion.

First of all, we understand from the Bible that repentance is granted from God, Himself and not when *man* wants to. We also understand that Judas was a reprobate and part of the unholy trinity. We have already seen that when a man becomes a reprobate, he has superceded every opportunity that he might have had to repent and receive forgiveness, for his soul. God at this point turns man over to Satan and pollutes his mind until the day he dies[1]. Jesus called Judas a Devil and the Son of Perdition. He was a two-faced liar his whole life and had the ability to deceive the best, but Jesus knew who he really was the whole time. When a man is a reprobate, he has no ability to go right and will go to any extreme to perform evil in the sight of God. We have seen that Judas blasphemed the Holy Ghost in the beginning of time, as part of the unholy trinity.

In the Book of Matthew 12:31-32 the Bible is clear that once this is achieved, there is no forgiveness in this world or the world to come. Mark 3:29 says that you are in danger of eternal damnation. When the unholy trinity blasphemed against the Holy Ghost, immediately God fulfilled that scripture and cast them into hell. As you can see, this is one major reason why Judas didn't repent God's way, because God would never deal with a reprobate. This also explains why Judas was never under conviction, as well.

Another reason why Judas failed to repent God's way was because of his destiny and all of the Bible prophesies that proclaimed he would betray the Lord. Judas was the Son of Perdition for a reason. His whole purpose in life according to the Bible was to betray the Lord for thirty pieces of silver. Think about it – if God would have given him the opportunity to repent and be saved, that would go against the scriptures that were already in place. Never before Matthew 27:3-4 do you find Judas being sorry for who he was or trying to show a humble spirit, but rather waited patiently for his time and sought to betray the Lord. It was only after he got caught that he ever showed any kind of remorse or grief. Remember, I said true repentance will change your life. When Judas died he went to his own place, showing us that he did not have the ability to exercise repentance by God. This is because he was a devil and it was never given to him. Why would Judas be sorry for completing what he came to do?

I also think of the statements that Jesus made concerning the life of Judas. Jesus was always exposing Judas and letting the people know that there was a devil among the crowd. Jesus said it would be good that Judas would never have been born, signifying his future judgement. He also gave him the title of the Son of Perdition or child of hell, even before he actually betrayed Him. He also called him the power of darkness and clarified that this was his hour, referring to his betrayal. Over and over again Jesus would tell his disciples that one of them would betray Him, referring to Judas. The entire time, Jesus knew the plan of God and that Judas was the one who would betray Him. He chose him anyhow in order to fulfill the Scriptures. Judas had just committed the worst sin ever committed in betraying the Son of God into the hands of sinners. When you think of all those factors, it would be foolish to think that Jesus would grant him repentance after all that Judas had done and all Jesus had said concerning him.

It is easy to see that Judas was there to be a thorn in the side of Jesus, to fulfill the Bible, and to betray the Son of God. Judas did not have the ability to repent the Bible way, and that is clear.

The reason I believe Judas repented himself was to cause even more confusion among those that viewed his life. Remember, the Devil is the author of confusion (found in I Corinthians 14:33), and his whole life was filled with lies and deception, up to this point. Why would this be any different? We know that it was impossible for this man to exercise Godly repentance[2], which is why that verse tells us that he repented himself. Judas was smart and he knew that this would be another way to deceive the people. Think about it – Judas was such a good pretender that, while at the Last Supper, Jesus plainly told his disciples that Judas was the one that would betray Him, and they still didn't believe Him. He had every one tricked, even the chosen eleven, through charisma and falsehood. Judas made everyone believe that he loved Jesus, when in reality he was sent to betray Him. He had already built a foundation and established the idea among the people that he loved Him. He knew that if he put on a show and appeared remorseful toward Jesus that he could make the people believe he was sorry and – that he truly did love the Savior. Judas was so wicked that he had every step of his mission planned out ahead of time and the people could not catch on to who he really was.

After his mission was complete, there was no more need for Judas. So, by suicide, he returns to his own place. The Devil has always been the master deceiver and a murderer from the beginning, and here we can see his title fulfilled in the life of Judas. So there you have some major reasons why Judas could not and would not repent the Bible way, simply because it was not in his power to do so.

---

[1] Romans 1:28
[2] Matthew 27:4

SATAN STOOD AT HIS RIGHT HAND

When I started to read through the Old Testament, I discovered that there is an amazing chapter that I wanted the world to see when thinking about the life of Judas Iscariot. In The Book of Psalms chapter 109, King David is referring to wicked men throughout this chapter explaining how their mouth is full of deceit and lies, and how they are fighting God without a cause. In verse 4, he talks about loving them and how they became His adversaries. In verse 5 He says they have rewarded me evil for good, and hatred for my love. Does that sound like Jesus and Judas or what? When you get to verse 6 through 8, you find a clear prediction of this man named Judas and what he would do in the future. These things are fulfilled exactly in the four gospels and in the book of Acts, being answered in the way that David predicted. Notice in verse 6 that the Bible says this wicked man will have Satan standing at his right hand. We understand that Satan entered into Judas and empowered him to perform evil in Luke 22:3 when he betrayed Jesus.

In verse 7, the Bible says to let him be condemned when he is judged and to let his prayer become sin. The Bible says in Matthew 27:3 that when Judas saw he was condemned he repented himself, but his prayer had no meaning because the chief priests and elders said unto him, "What is that to us, see thou to that." His prayer became sin, just as Psalms 109:7 said it would, for it fell on deaf ears and it caused him to throw down the thirty pieces of silver in the temple. He hung himself, just as the Bible said he would.

In verse 8 of Psalms 109, the Bible says "let his days be few; and let another take his office." We can clearly see in Acts 1:26 that Judas had a ministry of just three and a half years before his death, and his office went to another man by the name of Matthias. This fulfilled Psalms 109:8. In Psalms 109:11, the Bible says to let the extortioner catch all that he hath; and let the strangers spoil his labour. We find in Matthew 27:3-8 that all Judas stole and labored for did not satisfy. It went to strangers and extortioners, just like the Bible said it would. We find in Psalms 109:14-16 that his name shall be cut off because of his attitude and lack of mercy concerning the poor. We are aware of the fact that Judas got angry at a poor woman[1] for loving Jesus and trying to honor His Holy name. Jesus, in return, became offended toward Judas and clarified that she was poor and trying to do a good deed. He let money control his life and it was his demise. We understand from I Timothy 6:10 that "The love of money is the root of all evil: Which some have coveted after, and they have pierced themselves throughout with many sorrows." We know that Judas was very selfish and cared about nobody but himself, and he proved that throughout the Scriptures.

When we get to Psalms 109:17-20, the Bible speaks about the wicked being clothed with cursings and not blessings, and that because his soul hateth blessing to let it be far from him. In verse 18 the Bible declares that cursing will come into his bowels like water, and like oil into his bones. In verse 19 it says, "Let it be unto him as the garments that cover him, and for a girdle wherewith he is girded continually." In other words, let his shame remain with him forever. In verse 20, it says, "Let this be the reward of mine adversaries from the Lord, and of them that speak evil against my soul." In Acts 1:18 we find that Judas' reward of iniquity was a field of shame and defilement. We find that he fell headlong, burst asunder in the midst, and his bowels gushed out. When this moment happened, God was fulfilling Psalms 109, verses 1-20. He was showing us Judas' life of shame and disgrace. It's amazing that Judas fulfilled that whole chapter in the Old Testament, thus proving the Bible's perfection once again.

If you will read Acts 1:16 where Peter stood up to preach on the day of Pentecost, you will find that he will direct your minds back to this glorious chapter in the Bible. The apostle Peter clearly states in verse 16 that Judas was indeed the person who David was speaking of in Psalms 109. If you believe that this is a little far-fetched, then take it up with Peter and not me[2].

I think the most stunning thing about this whole chapter is the fact that in verse 6 of Psalms 109, Satan was at his right hand all the time. Once again we see the connection between Satan and this man named Judas Iscariot. Every move that Judas made was of a demonic design, and was worked to perfection with the help of Satan, himself. Jesus had so much to deal with and Judas was always undermining the Son of God. His motives were always evil and Psalms 109 proves that. No wonder Jesus called him a Devil in John 6:70. Judas was of that wicked one and his goal was accomplished as he fulfilled his title of the Son of Perdition by the Devil, himself.

I really hope that as we looked at Psalms 109, it helped us to realize the mindset of wicked men, and what their legacy will be when they die and leave this earth. Remember, this chapter deals with the nature of wicked men, and it perfectly describes Judas Iscariot.

I want to dwell on the fact that Satan stood at his right hand for a few of minutes. I believe the Bible is teaching us that Satan was helping Judas and empowering him the whole time. It is described how Jesus sits at God's right hand until He will make his enemies His footstool. One glad day, death will be defeated by Jesus[3]. The Lord is at the right hand of God making intercession for us according to the Book of Hebrews. While Jesus was on earth, God was always at his side encouraging Him to perform his mission and empowering Him to do so. The Bible teaches that Satan was at Judas' right hand, reminding him of his purpose and empowering him to do so as well. I believe that in the Book of John chapter 17 (when Jesus was praying to His Father and recapping His life and ministry), He was getting encouragement and approval for His perfectly performed plan. God was pleased with His Son, and Jesus was satisfied because He had pleased the Father.

I think Satan was also at the right hand of Judas, reminding him of his purpose and meaning in life. That's why Satan entered into him in Luke 22:3 because he was empowering him to fulfill his purpose when the time should come. When Jesus and Judas met in the Garden of Gethsemane directly after He prayed to the Father, Jesus was in the most powerful state of his ministry. Judas was as well because Satan had just entered into him. Jesus paints us a picture of the Tribulation Period and shows us exactly who will win this war after it is all said and done. Jesus said in John 18:5, "I am He," causing Satan and his crowd to fall upon the ground as a clear picture of Revelation 19:15 when the Antichrist is destroyed, by the Word of God.

Jesus is showing us by this example that His Father's right hand is stronger than Satan's right hand. When Jesus rose from the grave in Luke 24:1-6, He delivered a mortal wound to the head of Satan[4] and conquered death, hell, and the grave. This proved He is the King of Kings and Lord of Lords found in I Corinthians 15: 55-57. Praise be to Jesus, who giveth us the victory. God was telling us way back in Genesis 3:15 that one day Satan would use his son and his followers to hurt the Savior with a bruise to his heel. This would scar the Son of God and hurt Him deeply. However, God in return would use His Son and His crowd to deliver the knock-out punch when He rose from the dead[5]. The Word of God goes on to say that Jesus took the keys of death and hell, as well as the prisoners, and ascended back to heaven with His blood and forgiveness for all mankind. The Bible is clear that God eternally bruised the head of Satan, once and for all, proving that in the fight between good and evil, God will always be declared the winner.

There is yet another tie between Judas and the Antichrist in Psalms 109:6. We understand that the Antichrist will also be a Demon-possessed man that will have Satan at his right hand. Similarly, Judas was a man of destiny that Satan dwelled in to achieve his mission in betraying Jesus. The Antichrist will also be a predestinated man that Satan will indwell to help him carry out his master plan. His life is already determined, and it will surely come to pass exactly how the Bible said it would, much like Judas has already displayed in his ministry.

We understand that the Devil has a large following that he is leading through rebellion and disobedience to carry out his master plan. The blueprint is being laid out and the mystery of iniquity is already at work. Paul the apostle said that we, as Christians, are "… Fighting against principalities, and powers, against the rulers of the

darkness of this world, against spiritual wickedness in high places[6]."
In other words, Satan has sent his demons to influence his children
so that they might carry out his unholy deeds. The Devil is hard at
work using many different elements to bring them to pass. Satan
is using his children to set the stage for the Tribulation Period, just
like God uses His children to carry out His master plan. Satan never
quits and he has this world under his spell. When you look around
the society that we are living in today, you will find that we are a part
of the most vile and evil generation that has ever been recorded in
the history of mankind. Satan has people blinded to his true motives
and has leaders in authority that are performing his lifelong dream[7].
What's happening in Washington D.C. today is a perfect example.
They are hard at work destroying the Constitution, taking away the
freedoms that men and women bled and died for in the years gone
by. Our government is working hand in hand to bring in the one
world government that is a set-up of the Antichrist.

President Obama is being helped by demonic spirits and the cast
he has behind him is no different. They hate God, and they hate the

Bible. This country is filled with reprobates and heathens that support his agenda because they do not attend church and are ignorant of the Devil's devices[8]. Satan is using the hearts of men to make his plan accepted worldwide and it is happening right before our very eyes. With all that being said, Satan is using wickedness in high places and the rulers of darkness to help him complete his goal. When it comes to indwelling those people, however, he doesn't have to because he has his demons and powers at work to perform that duty. On the other hand, when it comes to Judas and the Antichrist, the Bible is clear that Satan, himself entered into them to help complete their task.

These are the only two men in which Satan has ever indwelt himself without the use of his helpers. Their mission is so important that Satan, himself entered into them so that they might fulfill their destiny. When it comes to the life of Judas and the Antichrist, you will always find the presence of Satan by their sides to guide and help them along the way. When you get a chance, read Psalms chapter 109 and you will see the sudden end of a wicked man. If you look closely you will see this man named Judas, and how he fulfilled

his destiny. The Bible is so amazing when you study it and realize

the truths that are in it.

---

[1] John 12:6-8
[2] II Peter 1:19-21
[3] Psalms 110:1
[4] Genesis 3:15
[5] Ephesians 4:8-10
[6] Ephesians 6:12
[7] II Corinthians 4:3-4
[8] II Corinthians 2:11

THE ROOT OF ALL EVIL

The subject that I want to cover in this particular chapter is the very thing that has destroyed the hearts and minds of untold millions – and even billions – of people throughout the course of history. It is the major problem that is corrupting our hearts today. The subject that I want to cover caused Satan, Judas, and the Antichrist all to fall because they allowed this sin to captivate and control their lives. I want to take a few minutes to talk about the love of money found in the Book of I Timothy 6:10. The Bible teaches that it is the root of all evil, and every other sin is a result of this one sin. Notice that it is not a sin to be blessed and to *have* money; it just becomes a sin when people start to *love* money. It seems like folks will go through any extreme to get it, no matter what it takes, or whom it hurts in the process. The Devil has this world wrapped up in plea-sure and satisfaction and it has been the downfall of all mankind.

Money has a way of changing good people into evil people more than anything else in this world. A good example of the love of money would have to be what has happened to America in the day in which we live. The Bible says in the Book of Psalms 9:17 that every nation which has forgotten God will be turned into Hell. This Biblical truth is happening right before our very eyes. God says in the Book of Matthew 6:24 that no man can serve both God and mammon. You will either serve God, or you will serve the Devil. God expects man to serve Him and to be in church everytime the doors are open. He also expects mankind to honor Him with their tithes and offerings that He has blessed them with throughout the course of their week, and to be faithful to His house. As a result, He will bless man and help him with their everyday life, guiding them every step of the way. This is what God has always intended for man to do since the beginning of time.

God wants man to walk and fellowship with Him in the cool of the day as he controls their life, and helps them along life's road. However, as we know, man has rebelled and wanted his own way. Feeble man began to rely on his own abilities and not God's to make it through life. The Bible shows us that we have never been able to recover, as humans, and we are now in worse shape than ever before. The United States of America is a perfect example of what I am talking about. There once was a day that America loved God and was faithful to Him. God in return sent His blessings and guided the leaders of this country in the paths of Righteousness. God guarded and protected this land because of their humble spirit and their God-filled attitude towards the things of Him. America used to be faithful to church, and even closed down places of business on Sundays because they had a respect for God and what He meant to their country. America used to have values and would help their fellow man because they put God first, family second, and self last. In our day, people have flipped this around and have put self first, family second, and God last. They hold money as their god instead of the Savior.

In days gone by, people would attend the House of God on Sunday and reject double-time that their jobs would offer them because they understood that without God, money isn't worth a dime. People feared God and would never miss church for personal gain or selfish motives because they believed their soul was more important than silver or gold. The Bible says in Mark 8:36, "What shall it profit a man if he gain the whole world and lose his own soul?" Most Americans use to believe that and would never work on Sunday. Let me say, those days are long gone.

People have allowed the Devil to detour their life away from the plan of God through the love of money and selfish desires. The Bible says in I Timothy 6:7 that we brought nothing into this world, and it is certain we can carry nothing out. Misery loves company and the Devil is a masterful deceiver. His whole goal is to get people to forget God through the love of money and greedy gain. He knows that people who are wrapped up in money will be so high and lifted up, and so concerned with building an empire, that when it comes time to die they will suddenly wake up in hell and have a life that is a failure when it is all said and done.

In Luke 12:16-21, you will find a man that worked hard his entire life to chase after the mighty dollar and to get ahead in life. We find that he forgot all about God and worked to be rich. This man had gained everything life had to offer and he had made money his god. The Bible tells us that he had to build the bigger barns just to store all the goods that he had attained in his life. This man was on top of the world and thought he had his whole life in front of him. The problem was God was not in the picture and Mr. Death had come to claim his next victim. The Bible calls him a "FOOL," and says in verse twenty-one that he that layeth up treasure for himself is not rich towards God. In other words, because his life was consumed by his love for money, his life was a waste in God's eyes. Jesus also said in Luke 18:25 that it is easier for a camel to go through an "eye of a needle," than for a rich man to enter into the Kingdom of God.

The Bible teaches that the love of money is the biggest tool that the Devil uses to corrupt the minds and hearts of people worldwide. Please, do not let money control your life. There have been times that I have begged people to come to church, over and over again, but they would refuse my offer because they had to work that overtime and get that money. This country as a whole stopped serving God a long time ago, and started serving money in His place. The people's desire for riches, at any cost, has caused America to fall and turn their backs on God many years ago. As a result, this has brought the judgement of God like never before. When you choose to take God out of anything, as a nation, you will have a mess on your hands.

America is just a shadow of what it used to be when it was great and honored God with every move it made. When America served God they would always pray about situations, and would always do what was right for the country – regardless of whether or not they were financially benefiting from that decision. They trusted God and always tried to do what was right for the people. That's why we, as a nation, wrote something called the Constitution, for the people and by the people. May I say that in the America we are living in today, this belief no longer exists. It seems as though every move America makes does not involve God, but always involves the LOVE OF MONEY.

This country is the greediest and most money hungry society that has ever existed in history. They threw God out of the picture many years ago and they could care less about anybody but themselves. It seems every move that this world makes has selfish intentions behind it. The love of money can be defined as some one always desiring what others have, and never being happy until they get it. Even after they get that thing, they are never going to be happy until they get something better, and so on and so forth. There is something about money that will leave you wanting more, and will leave you empty in your soul. Some of the happiest people I have ever met have been people that are not blessed with much, but are thankful for what they have. On the other hand, some of the saddest people I have met have been people that cheated and lied there way through life to gain the riches of this world. However achieving their goals only left them empty and dry.

The Bible teaches men to give and then they shall receive. God wants us to rely on Him and nothing else to make it in life, but most people rely on themselves – without God. Let me quickly say that those people will never be joyful in life, and will be empty and cold on the inside. The Bible says in Matthew 6:19-20,

"Lay not up for yourselves treasures upon earth, where moth and rust doth corrupt, and where thieves break through and steal:

But lay up for yourselves treasures in heaven, where neither moth nor rust doth corrupt, and where thieves do not break through nor steal:"

The Bible also tells us in Colossians 3:2 to set your affections on things above, not of things on the earth. The Word is teaching us that, with Jesus, you can be satisfied, but with Satan you will never be satisfied. I have seen people that love money and how they have let it turn them into an entirely different person. It has no doubt destroyed their lives. When I was a teenager I viewed a lot of different people's situations that were controlled by sin and money, and I saw how it ruined their future with the Lord. It was at that point where I made an important decision in my life. Around the age of eighteen, when I started working, I decided right there and then to never let the love of money change who I was. Even though I was tempted to spend that money on worldly pleasures, God led me to use that money to help different preachers around the country, and I began to store up treasures in heaven like the Bible says.

Let me tell you with all sincerity, that God in return filled me with the Holy Ghost and gave me a sustaining joy that this world just cannot give. I have seen friends covet after money and in return the Devil left them with nothing. Be very careful not to love the things of this world because you are living a life that is evil in the sight of God[1].

America is so spoiled that it is sickening. God has blessed this country with so much and in return it has turned its back on Him, and served itself. We are so privileged to live in this country and people think they deserve everything, while the rest of the world deserves nothing. The love of money has caused us to take for granted what God has given us through his sovereign grace. Please allow me to give you a good example of what I am talking about. I heard a famous preacher describe how God allowed him to visit the Philippines to preach the gospel unto those very poor people. He said many of those people had never owned a pair of shoes or a new shirt, or even eaten a candy bar in their whole life up to that point. The preacher went on to say that some of those people were fifteen to eighteen years old. Think about that.

We are so blessed to live in this country. The preacher continued by saying that every night when he would preach to those precious people, they would walk up to forty miles one way, bare-footed to hear the gospel of Jesus Christ. They did this knowing that after the preaching was over that they would walk another forty miles in the dark, back to their homes. The church was so poor that they didn't even have a church bus to pick up their members. This preacher said that thousands upon thousands of people would show up every night, and would be thankful for the chance to hear the bible, though they were poor, and had to walk home. This man of God said that those people were the most humble and nicest people that you would ever hope to meet. Those people had values, and could care less about earthly riches. On the other hand, that same preacher would preach in America where we are blessed with so much; and he would have, maybe, one hundred and fifty people show up to hear him on any given night.

In America, God has given us cars, good jobs, and all the comforts of life, yet we can't be faithful to the house of God. In contrast, the people of the Philippines had nothing and they were still happy and faithful to Christ. The love of money has ruined this great country and caused us to stray away from the values that built it in the first place.

America has served money for much too long now, and God is not pleased. This country hates the things of God and embraces the ways of the Devil. Everything America is about in these last days consists of money and personal gain. This has led its people down a path of no peace and no happiness. It is safe to say that America has sold its soul for a dollar.

There was a time in this country that America was self-sufficient and refused to rely on the help of any countries but itself. We leaned on our own resources and depended on the grace of God to make it day by day. The Bible teaches us to be content in whatsoever state we are in[2]. The Bible says Godliness with contentment is great gain in I Timothy 6:6. America was at its peak when they depended on God to supply all its needs. However, when America quit serving God and began serving the Devil, it started to turn from the ways of the Bible and turn unto the love of money. America started to rely on cheap labor from God-hating countries, and it has been the downfall of this great country. We are in the worse shape this nation has ever been in, and it is a direct result of its greed and its love of money. Just like I Timothy 6:10 teaches us, all sin stems from the love of money and this is proven by the actions of the United States of America. This country was blessed beyond measure when it believed the Bible and walked with God. However, when the Devil influenced the hearts of men through greed and the love of money, America went downhill in a hurry. America, through the love of money, has allowed sin beyond our imagination to enter its shores. Man once again has fallen into the hands of Satan.

What amazes me about this awful and terrible sin is the fact that Satan, Judas, and the Antichrist all fell by the exact same offense. We see through their lives that the love of money has always been the root of all evil. All three of these individuals were not satisfied with what they had, but always craved what God had. We need to remember once again that it is not a sin to have great riches, but it is only sin when it consumes your life.

We find, first of all, that Satan was created by God and enjoyed all the splendors of heaven. God had given him everything the world had to offer and designed him to live with Him for all eternity. The

Bible says in Ezekiel 28:15 that Satan was perfect from the creation until iniquity was found in him. The Devil had it "made in the shade drinking lemonade" when he obeyed God. However, as we know, his downfall occurred when he started to wonder what it would be like to be the top dog (so to speak), or when he wanted to exalt himself above God and have what He had. When Satan began to covet God's position and to be unthankful for what He had done for him that's when he was banished from heaven. Satan was sentenced to hell, along with one third of the angels of God. This sin is called the love of money and all other sins, from that point forward, was a result of what Satan exhibited in heaven. It is a mystery how someone that had it so well could screw it up so badly, ruining it for all mankind. We understand that the root of all evil began with greed and covetousness. This would have never happened if Satan would have just obeyed God in the first place.

Judas Iscariot also had the honor of being hand-picked by God, Himself for three and a half years as he followed the footprints of the Nazarene. Jesus was as good to Judas as anyone that ever lived.

Anything Judas needed, Jesus would give it to him. He watched Jesus heal the sick, raise the dead, calm every storm, preach like nobody had ever preached, performed miracles, and even let him take care of the funds. As long as Judas followed Jesus, his problems were forever gone and he would have everything he ever needed. There was a problem, however. Much like Satan craved merchandise in Ezekiel 28:16 and wanted everything God had, Judas loved money and it became his god. Judas proved this throughout his life, because Jesus said he was a thief. Even though Jesus gave him everything, he always wanted more and was never thankful in any circumstance.

Just like the Devil, his problem was on the inside where no one could see. Much like Satan, Judas disappointed God with his pride and coveting spirit, costing him his life. Man has fallen into the same trap for years and never seems to learn his lesson.

Thirdly and last of all, we see that this same sin will be the demise of the Antichrist, as well. We find a man who puts on a show for the first three and a half years of the Tribulation Period. He seems perfect to all mankind. After the three and a half years are up, we see that God removes this man's mask and reveals to the entire world who he was the whole time. The Antichrist, according to Daniel 11:37, will only be concerned with the following two things: self-gratification and his own will. We see the Devil at his all time high as he fulfills his lifetime mission of being praised by all that dwell on the earth. He will have the world at his mercy for a short period of time. He will control this earth by fear and submission. The Antichrist will seek the honor of men as he claims to be God. He will sit on David's throne during the last three and a half years of the Great Tribulation Period. This has always been the dream of Satan – to take over the world and to seemingly rule this universe. The good news is that there is only one God, and His name is Jesus Christ. He will handle this wicked crowd in the Battle of Armageddon and at the end of the Millennium, when Satan is thrown into the Lake of Fire.

Here we see another tie between Judas and the unholy trinity, and it is the love of money. What grew inside each one of these individuals was something called pride, as they all hated God and loved themselves. So we see that no matter how good God has been to us in our lives, we can take it for granted if we start to let the Devil fill our hearts with pride. We all have enough evil inside our hearts to rebel and turn away from the Lord. Let us learn from these three lives and never fall into the trap of thinking we're something when we are nothing. Without Jesus, we can do nothing. We are to follow Christ every step of the way if we want to make it through this life. It is so easy to get caught up with the affairs of this life, and the Devil will fight you every step of the way. Resist the Devil and he will flee from you[3]. Please let God control your life, and be careful not to make money your god.

I want to close this chapter by saying that from the beginning of time until the end, this has always been the downfall of man. We see the connection between these three men once again, as they all fall by the same exact sin. I hope we realize that this is not just by mere chance, but rather a pattern that we should really take note of when we think about the root of all evil in the lives of Satan, Judas and the Antichrist. They are one in the same and their lives prove it. I have come to the conclusion that if Judas could have a second chance to do it all over again, he would change nothing about his life. He would live his life exactly the same way because it was not his actions that necessarily caused him to fall, but rather his *nature* that caused him to fall.

Through this study, we understand that Judas had the exact same mindset as the unholy trinity and was just performing what was in his heart the whole time. Judas' problem was on the inside, and all other sins were just a by-product of his evil heart. He defined what pure evil is all about and it was his downfall throughout all eternity.

---

[1] I John 2:15-16
[2] Hebrews 13:5
[3] James 4:7

THE SON OF PERDITION

There is a term in the Bible that Jesus used to describe Judas which just can't be ignored. It is the term "Son of Perdition" found in John 17:12. This one statement is the major reason why I decided to go through with this study and go through the work that I have gone through. People that know me know that I try to live an honest life of truth and purity. The truth is that this statement "Son of Perdition" was quoted by none other than Jesus, Himself when it comes to describing Judas Iscariot. I can remember reading through my Bible and coming across this verse in John 17:12 and ignoring the terminology and this passage of scripture. After a while I came to the verse in II Thessalonians 2:3 where it also called the Antichrist the same thing. I thought to myself that it was a strange thing that Judas and the Antichrist are both labeled as the "Son of Perdition."

After thinking about it and studying these verses, I had to come to the conclusion that this was indeed the same person. Throughout this book we have seen that Judas is indeed one and the same (as the Antichrist), and that's why they are referred to in this way. I realized that denying the terminology of the 'Son of Perdition' would be wrong because I was disagreeing with God, Himself. Who am I to say that God is wrong and I am right if the Bible tells us that both of these men are the Son of Perdition? It forced me to realize that if I ignored the fact that Jesus called Judas the Son of Perdition, I would be lying to myself and that is something I didn't want to do. God knows I want to be honest with myself and everyone I come in contact with along life's road. The Bible says in the Book of I John 1:5 that God is light, and in Him is no darkness at all. In other words, every word of God in the Bible is true whether we want to believe it or not. He has no sin and cannot lie. See Hebrews 6:18-20 and Titus 1:2.

There is something I have been taught ever since I was a little boy growing up in church that is very important. I was always trained that when you try to talk to a sinner about their soul and you have an undeniable truth at your disposal from the Word of God, that you need to "camp on" (or stay on that verse), until that person can answer it. If you have a verse that is powerful and will get that sinner to see he is lost and needs Jesus, you never talk about anything else with them until they can answer the question that you are asking. I have seen my dad talk to people about the Bible and he would "camp on" a verse until they answered his question. Those people would get trapped and mad with my dad because they couldn't answer his question. They would try to talk about everything else under the sun and avoid it. When we are presented with truth from the Word of God, you are not meant to avoid it or explain it away. Rather, we are meant to believe it and to take it as truth, because it is the Word of God. The Bible says in the Book of I Timothy 1:4 that we should avoid people that minister questions and endless genealogies, or simply people that will not believe the Bible for *what* it says, and *who* is saying it. This terminology is called "camping around a verse" that is the truth, and demanding an explanation for those who are confronted by it.

When you look at the phrase "The Son of Perdition," you need to consider who said it and then read it over again. You will find that it was Jesus, and if you disagree with Him, then you have the problem (not God). Ask yourself over and over, "Why did Jesus make this statement when speaking about Judas?" I know when I practiced this procedure, it caused me to study and find the truth about Judas Iscariot. The fact that Jesus called him the Son of Perdition proves that he was full of sin from the start. The "Son of Perdition" means 'damnation', or 'child of hell.' The fact that Judas is labeled this title from the Bible will disprove a few theories or beliefs surrounding the life of Judas.

First of all, many Bible students and teachers believe that Judas loved Jesus and was his friend. They believe that through regret he betrayed the Son of God for thirty pieces of silver. People actually believe that Judas was a good man that, in time, turned his back on Jesus, and fell at the hands of pressure and temptation. I could not disagree more, and this term, the Son of Perdition, supports my beliefs. Jesus called Judas a devil and predicted that he would betray Him. Jesus was clear that Judas was not a true follower of Him, and proved it by labeling him the Son of Perdition in the Book of John 17:12. Jesus was letting the world know that he knew the blackness of Judas' heart, because He was God. In this phrase, the Son of Perdition, we have seen that it is defined as damnation. In other words, Judas was not able to perform good – only evil according to the Bible. His objective was to fulfill his purpose and to cause damnation to everyone he came in contact with.

Throughout His life, Jesus was clear that Judas was up to no good and he would one day betray Him. Judas was a reprobate, as we have seen, and was glad when his opportunity came to cause hurt to Jesus. He had no conscience and no feeling because he was the Son of Perdition. The term 'damnation' is found many times throughout the Bible, and in every circumstance it is talking either about hell, blackness, or pure evil. In Mark 3:29, the Bible tells us that damnation is the pure definition of darkness and hopelessness. When a man is a reprobate, he is hopeless in the mind of God and is evil in the sight of the Lord. Judas was a man full of damnation and spiritual blackness as he followed Jesus. Judas' actions promoted the Lord to call him the Power of Darkness in Luke 22:53, when the Lord was exposing his life. The term Son of Perdition rejects the theory that some hold that Judas loved Jesus, and made a mistake in betraying the Lord. Judas never loved Him, but always had the desire to betray Him because he was the Son of Perdition (according to Jesus' Word).

Secondly, another theory that is disproved by this term is one that is held by Bible scholars which believe that Judas became the Son of Perdition as a result of what he did when he betrayed the Savior. That is a false belief. The Bible tells us this in John 17:12 – when Jesus was praying to His Father – that He and the Father had already labeled Judas the Son of Perdition. This was long before his betrayal would happen in the ministry of Jesus. In this famous chapter, Jesus is discussing the relationship that He had with the

Father, before the world began. The Son of Perdition was a title that both the Son and the Father were comfortable with. It is strange that in this verse the Bible calls Judas the Son of Perdition, and not by his earthly name. The world knew him by Judas, but the Holy Trinity knew him as the Son of Perdition, even from the fall of Satan. If you don't believe that Judas was the Son of Perdition before John 17:12 or when Jesus was betrayed, then you would have to disregard the Old Testament verses that speak of him before he was born. David and Zachariah proclaimed that Judas would betray Him even before he was born and it came to pass, just as God said it would. They also talk about his future existence in the Tribulation Period, when he is breaking his covenant with all people as the Antichrist. Read Zachariah 11:10-14. You will see that he is the Son of Perdition in the Old Testament. Jesus was letting us know that Judas was the Son of Perdition even before he was born, in his earthly ministry according to the Old Testament. This can also be seen in Psalms, chapter 55. So we see that this theory is all blown to pieces as well, according to the Bible and the phrase, the "Son of Perdition."

The third theory that is refuted by this phrase and is held to by the majority of Christians is the idea that Judas could not be the Antichrist because he had already died, and once you die there is no coming back. If you know the Bible, that is certainly true with a normal man or woman. However, as we have seen, Judas is not a normal man, and he being the Son of Perdition proves that. We have seen that God has given only two men throughout the history of time this title and we have also seen that they are the same man. The reason this is true is because God said they were the Son of Perdition, not the *Sons* of Perdition. In other words, there are not two Sons of Perdition, but only one. God specified that Judas and the Antichrist are indeed the same man of destiny, and the rules are different for them because they are not normal men. They are that of an unholy trinity that must fulfill their purpose. We have seen that Judas and the Antichrist were straight out of hell and their life was determined before they were born.

As we have seen in the Tribulation Period, Moses and Elijah will appear as the two witnesses and will prophesy to any one that will listen during this time. Through God's power, they will preach in the darkest time there has ever been. God will use these two men greatly and Moses will come back from the dead to fulfill scripture.[1] When Jesus arose from the dead in the Book of Matthew 27:51-53, the Bible says that the graves were opened, and many bodies which slept (or were dead), arose after his resurrection and appeared unto many. If that scripture is correct, God said people that were dead already came back to life to fulfill scripture and appeared unto the Holy City. There is more. Recall John, chapter 11, when the family had gathered around the body of Lazarus. This man had been dead for four days before Jesus ever showed up at the grave. Jesus loved this family and he proves it by weeping over the situation in the book of John.[2] Jesus wanted to prove that he was the Resurrection and the Life to all of the people that were gathered around. Jesus says only three words, "Lazarus come forth," and Lazarus came back to life, with grave clothes and all. He appeared unto many and if you read the Book of John, chapter 12, you will find that Lazarus and Jesus are side by side at the table.

Another example that we should recall is found in the Book of Acts 9:36-41. It is here that we find a woman named Tabitha that was full of good works and alms deeds. The Bible says that she got sick, died, and they laid her in the upper chamber. The apostle Peter paid her a visit in which he kneeled down, prayed, then turned toward the body and said, "Tabitha, arise." The Bible goes on to say that she opened her eyes and sat up when she saw Peter. Once again we find some one that was dead, reappearing to display the will of God.

The last example I want to use is found in The Book of Acts 20:7-12, in the life of Paul. The Bible declares that Paul was a long-winded preacher and in chapter twenty we see that. In verse seven we read that on the first day of the week Paul expounded the Word of God unto them, and he preached until midnight. In other words, it was an all-day event. We see, in verse nine of this chapter, there was a young man named Eutychus that had fallen into a deep sleep and fell from the third loft, being taken up dead. The Bible says that Paul went to the man and fell on him to embrace him. Paul said unto the people, "Trouble not yourselves; for his life is in him." The Bible then records that only after Paul was come up again, had broken bread, and talked a long while (even until daybreak), they then brought the young man alive again, according to the Bible.

People need to study their Bibles and when they do, they will find that God can do whatever He wants when it comes to fulfilling Scripture. Jesus will use Judas again during the Tribulation Period to fulfill his title – The Son of Perdition – as we can see in the Book of II Thessalonians 2:3. We find in this verse that Judas had been dead for many years and is seemingly forgotten by most, but Paul restores his memory in this verse, as we can clearly see the future reappearance of Judas as the Antichrist. Most people have been taught that Judas could not reappear as the Antichrist because he had been dead for thousands of years. Remember, Jesus and Paul were the men who used the phrase, "The Son of Perdition," and who are we to disagree with them? As we have seen, God does not need our approval when it comes to His Divine Plan. To argue with these facts would be foolish and unwise. Judas will return again to fulfill his title, just as the Bible declares he will in II Thessalonians 2:3.

We see through this one phrase in the Books of John and II Thessalonians that it disproves three popular theories men and women hold on to when they think about Judas. The Bible teaches us in John 5:39 to search the scriptures. Be sure that what you are saying is Biblical and then give your belief. To ignore the term of Son of Perdition would be to ignore a great deal. It is an amazing phrase and one to take into consideration. The Bible says in Hebrews 4:12 that His Word is quick, powerful, and sharper than any two-edged sword, piercing your heart. It will come alive if you pay attention to it. Please let the Bible speak for itself and say what it means. When the Word says Judas is the Son of Perdition, then Judas is most definitely what the Bible says he is. When the Bible says that the Antichrist is also the Son of Perdition, then mark it down. They are one and the same.

To be honest, when God opened up the truth to me, I also was shocked and stunned; much like most of you probably are. What we must do is examine the Bible for ourselves and let God be true and every man a liar. Jesus was quoted as saying that it would have been good that Judas would have never been born, and that he was a devil. He also exposed him with being a thief, and the power of darkness. Judas was more than meets the eye, and the Bible is clear that he was of that wicked one the whole time. When you examine the title of the Son of Perdition, you will find an undeniable truth concerning Judas Iscariot that Jesus wanted us to discover. This is not a mistake and this is not a misprint. The Bible says in II Timothy 3:16 that "… All scripture is given by the inspiration of God," meaning all scripture is from God and is meant to be taken seriously.

My goal in showing you all these things about the Son of Perdition is to use the method that my dad would when he would "camp" around a verse, and focus on that one question until the other person would answer it. My question is to you, "WHY IS JUDAS CALLED THE SON OF PERDITION IF HE IS NOT THE ANTICHRIST?" My hope is that you will answer this question and let it dawn on you that Judas is the Antichrist, just like the Bible says he is. This was the sole purpose I wrote this book and I hope it changes your life, as it did mine. Many preachers will teach Judas in a different light, and I respect most preachers, but when it comes to Judas being the Antichrist or the Son of Perdition, I believe the Bible is clear that they are one and the same. If they choose to preach otherwise, they are spreading false doctrine and they need to change their view if they desire to line up with the Bible. I do not like sitting in church and hearing false doctrine, as a child of God. When it comes to the life of Judas, he is the most misunderstood man ever recorded in the Bible as far as preaching goes. The Word says in II Timothy 2:15 that Christians need to study to show themselves "approved unto God, a workman that needeth not to be ashamed," and notice, "...<u>Rightly dividing the Word of Truth.</u>"

My purpose in writing this book is to tell the truth about Judas and clear the air concerning this wicked and evil man. Jesus said that he is the Son of Perdition and if Jesus said it, then it is good enough for me. If I were wrong I would admit it, but if I am right then most people are wrong about the Son of Perdition. I sure hope through this study that you will quickly change your mind. Thank you for reading this portion of the book and I trust it has shed some light on Judas, the Son of Perdition. The verses that I have chosen to closeout this chapter with are found in the Book of Revelations 22:18-19, where the Bible warns us not to question or change His written words that are recorded in heaven or there will be a price to pay. Many people pick and choose what they like in the Bible, and have even set out to change it because they disagree with what it says. There are hundreds of new bibles that have come on the scene in the last seventy or eighty years. They were changed and so-called 'corrected,' or are suppose to be easier to read, because people disobey the Word of God by changing what God has never intended to be changed. The problem with this is the fact that God said in Revelation 22:18-19 that adding to or taking away from the prophecies that are written in the Book will add all the plagues of the Word of God unto your life. You will be forever cursed from that day forward.

God's Word was never meant to be changed, but was meant to be believed. God is not the author of confusion, but the Devil is.

When you come across a verse in the Bible that you don't understand, please don't change it. Just ask the Lord to help you understand it and believe it by faith. When it comes to John 17:12 and II Thessalonians 2:3, I hope you will have an open mind and take the Lord at his word when it speaks of the Son of Perdition.

---

[1] Revelation 11
[2] John 11:35

THE CONCLUSION

In conclusion, I want to thank everyone that purchased a copy of this book from the bottom of my heart. I have tried, to the best of my ability, to expose the life of Judas Iscariot for what he always was. With this book I wanted to use as much Bible as I possibly could, and as little of my own opinion as humanly possible. There are many other factors concerning the life of Judas that could have been expressed, but it would have merely been speculation and the opinion of man. I tried to avoid that and simply give you the facts. What amazed me about this subject is the fact that there is very little said about the life of Judas or the Antichrist throughout the pages of the Bible. God, however, was gracious and gave me endless truths when it came to the identity of this man. Some of the material God showed me about Judas Iscariot was very shocking and revealing. When I started to view his life, and break down his true meaning, it was eye opening to say the least. Some of the verses and facts about this man were undeniable. I want to thank you personally for reading this book with an open mind.

Many people have a preconceived idea of who they believe the Antichrist is, but most of those people have no Bible to back it up. If you were taught like me, you were taught that Judas could not be the Antichrist for many different reasons. However, as we have seen, if the theory does not line up with the Bible, then you are wrong. I realize that most of the information presented to you was probably stunning and very different than the concept you might have had about Judas. Let me say, to the best of my ability I tried to give you facts from the Word of God. Judas was the Devil in disguise and I sure hope, after our in-depth view of his life, you have come to the same conclusion. My job is to present truth the best way I know how and your job is to determine whether this information is correct.

In my final statements, I want to discuss two very important topics concerning the life of Judas. I think it would be a shame after the study that we had, not to talk about the life Judas lived, and what it should teach us.

When I sit back and think about the life Judas lived, I believe God is giving us a clear message that He wanted us to take hold of. Judas Iscariot was one of the only men in history that was hand picked by the Son of God. Judas was very fortunate in the fact that he followed Jesus Himself, on a daily basis for three and a half years. He had the opportunity to learn from the best and follow God Himself. Judas saw every miracle Jesus performed, every storm He calmed, and every preaching sermon that Jesus spoke. He was even baptized in John 3:22 and John 4:2 by Jesus, Himself. The Bible teaches that he was given the power to perform miracles himself, in the days following Jesus. Judas was also given the honor of being the treasurer of God's church in his lifetime as well. In other words, he had Jesus at his service for three and a half years, whenever he wanted. Judas was able to do whatever the other eleven disciples did, as they followed the footsteps of Jesus. Judas was seemingly perfect in the eyes of men and had the whole world deceived. The problem that Judas had is the one that a lot of people have. He knew all about Jesus in his head, and he knew nothing about Jesus in his heart. He had all mankind deceived, but God knew his heart the whole time.

God was simply showing us in the life of Judas that if you have never been born-again, then you will never go to heaven when you leave this world. Think about it - Judas was baptized by Jesus Himself, yet he died and went to hell. Please allow me to take a few minutes and prove to you, from the Word of God, that Judas was indeed baptized by Christ. This has been an on-going debate among Christians over the fact of Jesus baptizing anyone during His earthly ministry. People believe that Jesus never baptized anyone during this time because of a verse in John 4:2. In this verse, the Bible says that Jesus baptized not, but His disciples. People will take that verse and run with it to prove that Jesus never baptized, only His disciples did. Let me say that they are taking that verse completely out of context because of John 3:22 and John 3:26. In these verses, the Bible clearly teaches that Jesus took His disciples only into the land of Judaea, tarried with them, and baptized His disciples. However, because of His fame and rapid popularity, people began to view this once in a lifetime sight of Jesus baptizing His disciples and word spread quickly. In verse twenty-six, the people told John that the man "whom thou barest witness to," was also baptizing, and all men come to Him. Notice that there is no mention of His disciples baptizing, only Jesus. John the Baptist responded by donating the rest of this chapter in celebration of Jesus and describing to the people that this was indeed the Messiah, who he was proclaiming all the time.

Let me ask you a question. If Jesus never baptized anyone in His ministry, then why did John 3:22 and John 3:26 tell us that he did? What John 4:2 is telling us is that Jesus only baptized one time, and one time only. In other words, no one was baptized by Jesus Himself, except His disciples. When people read that verse and say that Jesus never baptized, they are misquoting that verse. If you were to study your Bible in great depth, you would find that Christ only baptized one time according to John, chapter three. No where else in the other three gospels or any of the rest of Scripture does it ever record Jesus baptizing in any single passage. The Holy Ghost made it clear that Christ's ministry was to preach good tidings unto the meek, heal the broken-hearted, proclaim liberty to the captives, open the prison to those that are bound, and to proclaim the acceptable year of the Lord, according to the Book of Isaiah 61:1-2. John, however, was sent to baptize and prepare the way of the Lord. Jesus didn't come to baptize; that was John's job. You will never find anyone being baptized by Jesus, besides His hand-picked disciples in John, chapter three. Jesus did not want to rally his ministry around baptism, just salvation and forgiveness. What John 4:2 is teaching us is that Jesus, Himself never baptized anyone that was gathered to see Him that day or any other day, but only His chosen disciples. Let me clearly express once again that never before or after these verses will you ever find Jesus baptizing anyone else but His disciples. To deny that Jesus ever baptized anyone would be false and non-scriptural according to the gospel of John, chapter three.

We must conclude, by the Word of God, that Judas (being one of the twelve), was no doubt baptized by Jesus according to John 3:22 and John 3:26. As far as the scriptures are concerned, this was only mentioned one time in the Bible because Jesus wanted everyone to understand that it was a one-time event in His ministry. Never again would He baptize anybody except his chosen few. I just wanted to explain this subject in great detail and show you that Judas, in his lifetime, was baptized by Christ, Himself.

We also conclude that Judas did miracles and healed the sick, yet went to hell. Judas knew about Jesus as well as anyone that ever lived, but he is in hell today. Judas lived a seemingly good life in the sight of men, but the sad fact is he went to hell. Judas was even the treasurer and one of Christ's disciples, but was unsaved. God plainly is telling us through the life of Judas Iscariot that you may have an experience with God, may have the power to perform miracles, perhaps have been baptized, and are a good person. If, however, you have never been under conviction, repented of your sin, and confessed Jesus as your Savior, then you will make the mistake that many do and die without Jesus, opening your eyes in hell. This is exactly the pattern that the Devil is using today and will use during the Tribulation Period. The Bible declares that the Antichrist will capture the minds and hearts of the people through lying wonders and miracles. He will have the power to do everything that Judas did, but he will be lost as well.

When you talk to people today about their salvation and how they know they are going to heaven, many times they will bring up some phenomenal experience or miracle they have encountered (much like the Jews seeking for signs and wonders). It is no different in our generation. The Devil has people wrapped up in everything and anything religiously but, much like Judas, they will bypass the cross and will end up in hell.

I think about Noah, for example. This man of God was a preacher of righteousness for over one hundred and twenty years. In other words, he was a hell, fire, and brimstone preacher. Noah would pour his heart out and preach doctrine to all that would hear. People would disregard everything he had to say and laugh at his old-fashioned preaching. He preached that judgement was coming and they needed to repent. What is amazing about Noah is that he preached year after year, warning the people to get in the ark, and literally nobody believed him except his family. Only eight people got on the ark and avoided the judgement of God. It is no different in our day. If you look around this country, there are churches popping up everywhere, on a daily basis that promote love, unity, and miracles but have nothing to do with doctrine. You can find these kinds of churches everywhere you look. However, if you set out to find a church that believes like Noah and will tell you the truth of being a sinner, how Jesus is the only Way, and uses the King James Bible (1611), as the Word of God, let me tell you from experience - you will have to drive hundreds and hundreds of miles until you find one. In the end times the major tool that the Devil will use to get everybody to forget doctrine and to all get together in one accord to 'love' each other is something called miracles and lying wonders.

Let me quickly share with you something that God showed me about the last days and reveal to you just how few people in our generation are prepared to meet God when Jesus comes again. In Luke 17:26-28 Jesus compared this generation with that of Noah and Lot's by saying, "As it was in the days of Noah, and as it was in the days of Lot, so shall it be in the days of the coming of the Son of Man." Think about it. In Noah's day, only eight people were saved. In Lot's day, only four people were saved. When you think of it that way, how many people are actually saved in this generation? I did a study one time, eliminating all the false religions and false doctrines of our day, because I wanted a good idea of how many people were going to heaven in this generation. I came to the conclusion that 0.7% of the world is really going to heaven. So many people have religion, like Judas did, but they do not have redemption, like Peter did. Jesus said in the Book of Matthew[1] that few there be that find it (referring to heaven), but many there be that go in there at (referring to hell). The Bible also says in John 5:39 to "Search the scriptures, for in them ye think ye have eternal life." The Bible declares in II Corinthians 13:5 that you need to examine yourself whether you be in the faith. I talk to so many people about their souls, telling them that they have to be born again if they want to go to heaven when they die, and their response so often is that they could care less what the Bible says because they 'know what happened to them.' What they are basically telling you is that the Bible is false and their experiences are true. God said, "Let God be true and every man a liar."

If your salvation does not line up exactly with the Bible, then you are going down the wrong way and you need to turn around. I will not deny the fact that people can perform miracles by the spirit, but my question is – "What spirit are they doing it by?" The Bible says, "Try the spirits whether they be of God" in the Book of I John 4:1. In other words, match those spirits up to the Bible and if they do not line up, then they are of Satan. There are many false prophets that are after one thing – money. They will do anything in their power to use people for selfish reasons, much like the modern day TV evangelists and much like Judas and the Antichrist. Many of these false preachers are filled with Demons that have the ability to perform great miracles, but it is for selfish reasons and not the glory of God. In II Peter 2:1-5 we find that these false prophets are out to bring in damnable heresies and are simply using their followers for nothing other than money.

Let us use the life of Judas as an example in our lives. If you are in a church that promotes this kind of teaching that is all about miracles and not "offending" people, you better take a good look at the story of Judas and get away from that church. Remember, Judas is a prime example of being so close to Jesus, but in reality being so far away. If you have never been saved the Bible way, please get saved today.

The second thing I want to expound on about the life of Judas is the fact that Jesus (along with other great men found in the Bible) was the very men that made the statements about Judas, not me. One thing that I want to express to all who might read this book is the fact that if it was mainly my opinion, and not the Bible, then I could see how you may have problems with much of the material written within this book.. However, because it is the very Word of God, there is really no debate as far as I'm concerned. The King James (1611 A.D.) Bible is perfect in every way and it has no errors. Men have set out to destroy the Bible for years and have failed every time. The Bible says in II Timothy 3:16 that "All scripture is given by inspiration of God." A statement that is made in the Bible should always be taken as correct. Bible prophesies are being fulfilled on a daily basis and can be seen every day. I have always heard the saying that "God said it, I believe it, and that settles it." The fact of the matter is whether you believe it or not doesn't change the fact that it is settled in the mind of God. I just taught a lesson on the subject, "Things that prove the Bible is real."

In this study, God gave me so many things that we can see on a daily basis to prove that His Word is true. For example, back in Genesis 9:12-17 God had destroyed the world by the flood. As a result, God made a covenant with mankind that he would never destroy the world again by a flood. He also caused a rainbow to appear in the sky to prove to man that He was serious about what He said. The next time it rains, look outside and you will see the fulfillment of that scripture.

Another thing that proves the Bible is real is in Matthew 24:32-34. It foretells Israel becoming a nation again and that the generation to see it will see all things come to pass. We understand that in 1948 Israel became a nation and proved the Bible once again.

The Bible also teaches us that just as heaven is real, there is a place called hell that enlarges herself every day (found in Isaiah 5:14). Hell is just as real as the nose on your face. I taught the kids that there was a man by the name of Dr. Assacoff that wanted to dig to the center of the earth to see what he would find. Dr. Assacoff was an atheist and rejected even the thought of God. The story is told that he was digging in Siberia to the center of the earth. When his team drilled nine miles down their tools started to break and refused to work. That's when they started to hear voices of human souls. Matthew 12:40 teaches us that hell is in the heart of the earth, or roughly thirteen miles under your feet. This discovery changed Dr. Assacoff's view on hell and he decided to record his findings the best way he knew how. Dr. Assacoff closed his investigation and stopped their goal of drilling to the center of the earth. He was afraid that if he released his findings to the public of what was down there, it would haunt him until the day he died. He decided to keep silent concerning this issue. When he died, his son received access of all of his father's recordings. His son then chose to release the findings to the public for everyone to hear.

What you will hear, if you decide to listen to it, are actual voices of people screaming in the pits of hell. You will also hear the sounds of demons and other sounds of hell. There is only thirty seconds of these sounds found on the internet, but there are hours of this in the possession of Dr. Assacoff's recordings. This proves the Bible once again.

There are so many things just like these three examples found throughout the Word of God that prove that the Bible is true. My point simply is whether we believe the Bible or not does not make a difference in the mind of God. The things that are recorded about Judas had to come true just like the Bible said, or it would be false. Judas fulfilled all that was written of him because the Bible is true. Remember how I said in my introduction that you should question the opinion of man, but believe the Word of God. This book is an example of God's final stamp of authority on the life of Judas, and the fact that he is the Son of Perdition.

This has been an amazing study and one that I hope you have enjoyed. I want to tell you in closing that if you know the Bible at all, you understand that Jesus could come back today and nothing is holding Him back. Everything concerning Bible prophecy has already been fulfilled and we are in the last of the last days. If you read in Matthew- chapter 24, Mark-chapter 13, and also II Timothy- chapter 3 (speaking of the last days), you will find that it is like reading the daily news. We are so close to Jesus returning, in the rapture of the church, it is scary. Whether you believe this book or not and whether you believe the Bible or not, will not change the fact that it is true. I have been in church my whole life and I am seeing things today that are so amazing concerning the Bible. Sinner friend, I beg you to consider your salvation and give Jesus a chance in your life. Remember that Jesus had 12 members in His church and one of them was a Devil.

The majority of this world is lost because they are not willing to do what the Bible says. Please do not make this same mistake. I sure hope you will consider your eternity and say to yourself, "Do I really know that I have been born again the Bible way, by the Spirit of God?" Jesus may be calling you right now to come to Him for salvation. My advice would be not to fight Him but to accept Him when you have a chance to receive him. God said in Genesis 6:3, "...My spirit shall not always strive with man." God is not going to speak with a man or woman forever when it comes to salvation, but will deal with him a certain number of times in his life. If a man refuses the calling of God enough, God will leave that person alone and deal with somebody else.

John 3:8 compares salvation to the wind. Jesus said, "The wind bloweth where it listeth and thou hearest the sound thereof, but canst not tell whence it cometh or whether it goeth: so is every one that is born of the Spirit." Jesus was telling us that salvation is like the wind and, much like the wind, it will come when it wants to and leave when it wants to. In other words, God will speak to mankind when he chooses to and if mankind refuses to accept this invitation, He is not obligated to speak to their heart again.

There are over six billion people in this world today, and over four billion have never heard the name of Jesus Christ in their native tongue. It would be foolish to think that God will deal with your heart over and over again when most of the world has never heard the gospel even once. The Bible says in John 6:37 that he will in no wise cast you out. If you come to Jesus with a humble spirit and a heart full of repentance, admitting that you are lost, asking Jesus to forgive you, and to take you to heaven when you die, then God will hear your prayer and redeem your soul. It is that simple.

The Bible records in I John 5:13 that you can <u>know</u> that you are going to heaven through what Jesus did on the cross. In Romans 10:9-10 the Bible says all you have to do is "confess with your mouth the Lord Jesus, and believe in your heart that God hath raised Him from the dead" and God will save your soul. If you are lost, harden not your heart[2], but rather open it up so that Jesus can come in. The more you refuse his call, the worse the situation will become. Some may believe that they are good enough to get to heaven and that they can make it on their own without the help of Jesus. Let me say in love that you are making a big mistake.

Think about this – if we were good enough to get to heaven, then why did Jesus come and die? He came to die because he was the Savior and we are the sinners. Unless we accept this offer that Jesus has made to all mankind, we will remain a sinner and separated from the presence of God. Jesus has shed his blood and rose from the dead so that you and I could be in heaven for all eternity. Let me say with all due respect that you would be a fool to reject the Son of God and all he has done. The only way to heaven is through Jesus found in John 14:6. If you try to get there any other way, you will come up short.

The final statement that I want to make in closing this book is simply this. You may know all about Jesus in your head, but do you know Jesus in your heart? Don't be like so many and miss heaven by eighteen inches (the distance between the head and the heart). What I mean by that is if Jesus speaks to your heart, don't over think it.

Just accept it. Too many people overcomplicate it and make it hard. God is looking for a humble heart and a child-like faith to believe the Bible and accept the Savior. Those who know me know that I take the Bible very seriously, and I would never lead you astray. Jesus loves you and proved it by dying in your place. If you never receive His free gift[3], then you will only be *acquainted with* Jesus but will never really *know* Him. I love you so much, and I hope you enjoyed the ride. God bless you.

----

[1] Matthew 7:13-14
[2] Hebrews 3:8
[3] Romans 6:23

LaVergne, TN USA
14 November 2010
204781LV00003B/5/P